T5-CVF-594

JUN 0 8 1992

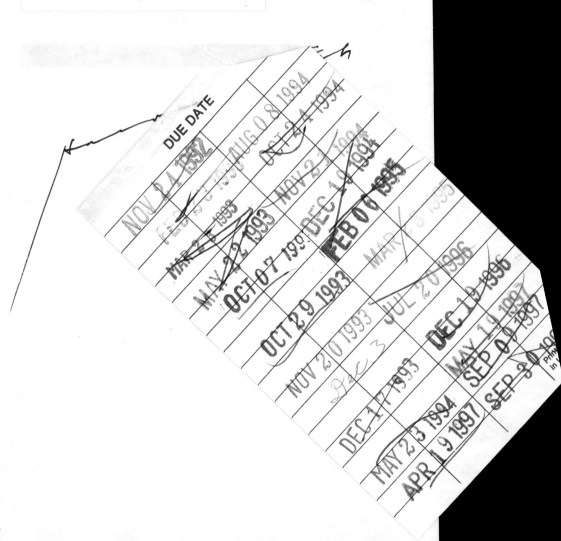

DUE DATE

NOV 24 1992
FEB 0 5 1993
MAR 2 5 1993
AUG 0 8 1994
OCT 2 4 1994
NOV 2 3 1994
DEC 1 0 1994
MAY 2 2 1993
OCT 0 7 199
DEC 1 199
FEB 0 6 199
MAR 2 9 199
OCT 2 9 1993
NOV 2 0 1993
JUL 2 0 1996
DEC 1 9 1996
DEC 1 7 1993
Dec 3
DEC 1 9 1996
MAY 1 6 1997
SEP 0 9 1997
MAY 2 3 1994
APR 1 9 1997
SEP 3

WILL ROGERS, A BOY'S LIFE

Books by Harold Keith

WILL ROGERS, A BOY'S LIFE

SHOTGUN SHAW

A PAIR OF CAPTAINS

BRIEF GARLAND

GO, RED, GO!

THE BLUEJAY BOARDERS

THE RUNT OF ROGERS SCHOOL

SPORTS AND GAMES

RIFLES FOR WATIE

FORTY SEVEN STRAIGHT

OKLAHOMA KICKOFF

SUSY'S SCOUNDREL

KOMANTCIA

THE OBSTINATE LAND

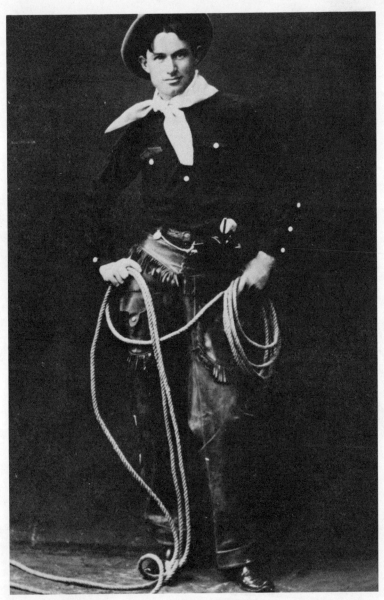
(Courtesy Will Rogers Memorial and Birthplace)

Will Rogers, A Boy's Life

By HAROLD KEITH

ILLUSTRATED BY
KARL S. WOERNER

LEVITE OF APACHE
PUBLISHER - - - NORMAN, OKLAHOMA

Originally published by Thomas Y. Crowell Company, 1937
Revised edition by Levite of Apache, 1991
Copyright 1991 by Harold Keith

ISBN 0-927562-08-1
ISBN 0-927562-09-X Pbk

Printed in the United States of America
by the Transcript Press, Norman, Oklahoma
Library of Congress Catalogue Card No. 91-62354

To
Virginia
with Love

FOREWORD

THIS BOOK is pointed at Mr. Rogers' boyhood and youth through his early twenties. The first four-fifths of it deals with that. I have tried to project him against the background of his own Cherokee country, the influence of his parents, particularly his mother, and the environment of his times. To find and develop traits in the youth of this native Oklahoman that the Nation would know and like so well in his adult life—his friendliness, honesty, sensitiveness, humor, philanthropy, courage, sanity, shrewdness, decency, his great love for horses, cattle, roping, everything pertaining to ranch life, and the fact that regardless of the rigid highway that schools and a gruff but well-meaning father tried to send him along, he always had to travel his own road.

Although his father, who was a man of considerable means and a believer in education, sent him to six different schools in a day when good schools were scarce, the boy Will Rogers wasn't interested in any of them, yet acquired a wide practical education and lived to be known and loved and honored all over the world. When a friend once chided him about his lack of

FOREWORD

grammar, Rogers grinned and said: "Shucks, I didn't know they was buyin' grammar now days. I kinda figured maybe it was thoughts and ideas."

He helped steady millions of drifting people, not only financially through his charity campaigns and his own large personal gifts which he always tried to hide from public knowledge, but mentally and morally as well through his ability to lift people, guide them, make them laugh, and then make them think. Presidents, cowboys, financiers, Indians, kings, show people, children—he knew and liked them all and all were genuinely sorry when he died. I think—because of this personal trait which Lincoln had—that Will Rogers is one of the very greatest men who ever lived.

Source material for this book was gathered chiefly from the hundreds of Rogers' relatives and friends whom the author saw personally in the spring and summer of 1936. Their own reminiscences have been buttressed by a careful study of books, magazines, newspapers—everything I could find that Will Rogers had written and everything written about him.

The personal sources of my information have been so invaluable that it would require a long list of names to cover fully. However, I am appending a partial list of acknowledgments which must suffice in some measure to express my appreciation and thanks.

H. K.

University of Oklahoma,
July 1, 1937.
Revised Edition October 1991

CONTENTS

WILL ROGERS, A BOY'S LIFE

YOUNG WILL VISITS KEMPER TO SEE HIS FORMER ROOMMATE,
JOHN PAYNE

Chapter 1
THE PARENTS OF WILL ROGERS

O F ALL the Indian tribes that lived in the mountains and plains of North America in the early
days of our country, few equaled in militant strength,
in agricultural wealth, or in real culture the great
Cherokee nation. Their lands covered more than forty
thousand square miles; rich miles filled with game and
fish; fertile miles planted to apples, melons and maize.
For centuries the Cherokees had owned vast areas in
Tennessee, Georgia, Alabama, and the Carolinas and,
by treaty, were recognized as an independent nation.
The entire tribe could read and write, thanks to
Sequoyah's invention of the Cherokee alphabet, and
they had their own school system and published a
newspaper.

Then, in 1838, was written one of the ugliest chapters in our history—the story of the Cherokee removal.
The United States Government, realizing the vast
mineral resources of the Cherokee lands, drove the
Indians into the Indian Territory and turned their
property over to the white men.

A portion of the tribe accepted this fate quietly,

signed a treaty of removal, and went voluntarily to new homes in Arkansas and the Indian Territory, but there were others who resisted bitterly and left their lands only when driven out.

Thousands—possibly a fourth of the Cherokee nation—died on the march, but the survivors, under their chief, John Ross, settled in the Indian Territory and set up their government with Tahlequah as the capital.

In those days the Indian Territory covered about twice the area of the present state of Oklahoma. It was a savage land teeming with wild life. Great flocks of green parakeets drifted over the bottom lands feeding on the sycamore balls there; wild turkeys and geese gobbled and honked from the prairies and marshes; and among the blue stem grass that grew to the height of a deer's shoulders, quail and prairie chickens were as thick as black birds. Here too skulked the black wolf, a constant menace to man and beast. There were few roads and fewer towns. The Cherokees gave musical names to their settlements, such as Oowala, Talala, Cooweescoowee, and, of course, the capital, Tahlequah.

Though desperately handicapped by lack of capital and tools, the transplanted Cherokees worked so intelligently that in little more than twenty years after coming into the new land they were again prosperous, owning four thousand slaves, two hundred thousand head of cattle, more than one million hogs, and twenty-five thousand horses.

More than that, these enterprising people, with no expense to the Federal Government, built a sound school system, establishing forty common schools and two high schools or seminaries within the boundaries of their nation. In 1907, when the Indian Territory became a part of the new state of Oklahoma, the tribe disbanded and became citizens of the United States. The Cherokee Nation had ceased to exist, but what a fine heritage of bravery and high honor it left to the men and women who were to be its descendants!

Among the Old Settlers were Robert Rogers—of Irish and Scotch descent—and his wife Sally Van Rogers, and to them on the eleventh of January, 1839, was born a son whom they named Clem. Among the group of Cherokees who had resisted the Federal Government were Martin Matthew Schrimsher, a Welshman, and his wife Elizabeth Hunt Schrimsher, and to them, on October ninth of the same year, was born a daughter whom they called Mary. This boy and girl born in the Indian Territory in the same year, were the Clem and Mary who would later become the parents of Will Rogers.

Although these two children grew up within a comparatively short distance of each other, they never met until they were sent to school at the seminaries in

Tahlequah. Their parents—on both sides—were about one-quarter Cherokee, well-to-do, hard working, and eager that their children should have the best.

However, in spite of his parents' ambition for him, Clem Rogers made short work of his school days. He attended school at the Baptist Mission for three terms and then went to the Cherokee Male Seminary at Tahlequah. But at the first possible moment he gave it up to take a job driving cattle on the range for Joel M. Bryan, a wealthy man of that country who owned thousands of head of cattle and several trading posts.

Clem was a strapping, well-knit young fellow—a hard worker, a good rider and an excellent shot. When necessary he could—and did—use his fists. While he was still a boy his father died and his mother subsequently married a man named William Musgrove. He and Clem were the best of friends, and when the younger man showed signs of becoming a shrewd business man with ambitions to possess his own herd and ranch house, it was William who helped him with his plans.

Clem had decided to settle in the wild Cooweescoowee country in the western part of the Territory. Here was virgin soil and the finest grass within the Nation's border; so, with his mother's generous gift of a herd of twenty-five cows and a bull, some ponies, and two Negro slaves, Rab and Houston, he set out.

With William Musgrove's help he built a sturdy ranch house. Here he hoped to bring as his bride pretty Mary Schrimsher, whom he had been courting since their meeting in Tahlequah, during Clem's short stay at the seminary there.

Not satisfied with cattle-raising alone, he set up a trading post and store beside the little creek which was to be known as "Rab's Creek." Although the settlers were scattered and travelers few—chiefly Osage Indians from their reservation in Kansas—his store and trading post prospered and his herd grew. Now, Clem felt, he had something to offer a wife.

The plantation of Mary Schrimsher's father, seven miles from Tahlequah, was one of the finest in that part of the country, and from her earliest memory the little girl was surrounded with all the things that mothers and fathers love to give their children. On both sides of her family there had been men of prominence—two governors, a member of the state supreme court, congressmen. In the Cherokee Nation alone her people had helped draft every treaty that was made.

Sweet and unspoiled, Mary was a favorite with everyone. She first went to school at the Academy at Cane Hill, Arkansas, where all the wealthy Cherokee children were sent. Later she attended the Cherokee Female Seminary at Tahlequah, where she studied piano and voice in addition to the regular course. She was especially fond of music and was fortunate in having for her teacher a Russian noblewoman of exceptional talent, who had been banished from her native country.

Mary not only played and sang well, but she loved to dance too, and no party really began until she arrived. Nor did she forget the graver things, for she joined the Methodist Episcopal Church South, sang in its choir and became active in church work.

About this time the young ranchman, Clem Rogers, came courting her, and in 1858 they were married and went to live in the little ranch house in the wild Cooweescoowee country. If at first the lonely miles stretching on all sides frightened her, she was careful to keep it to herself, and because she was so gay and sweet and courageous, people for miles around loved to come to the Rogers home. Before long Mary felt herself an integral part of the new country which she was learning to like so sincerely.

For two years life in the little ranch house on Rab's Creek ran along smoothly. Clem worked from morning to night with his herd, and his store, and Mary busied herself with her household duties. They were young and happy and full of ambition. Life stretched out before them as sunny as the prairie itself.

Then, in 1860 came the first rumblings of war. John Ross, chief of the Cherokees, did his best to keep his people neutral in this new crisis. But unfortunately for the Cherokees, the very position of their lands made neutrality impossible. Their fruitful country soon became a battle ground for both the Union and Confederate armies, and they were forced, from military necessity, to side with one or the other.

Much of the Nation soon allied itself with the Confederate cause. The Indians were Southerners by birth, ancestry and environment. Many of them were slave holders and had large amounts of their trust funds invested in Southern securities.

Clem Rogers believed sincerely that the South was in the right. He rushed Mary to her people at the old plantation in Tahlequah, and then he himself rode hard to Fort Wayne in the Delaware district where in July, 1861, he joined the Confederate cause. He knew the war would ruin him. His little ranch and herd of cattle lay just sixty miles from the Kansas border, right in the path of the Union army, and this meant his herd was doomed. But he had a steady, unwavering courage. His loyalty, as he saw it, was with the South.

From the first he distinguished himself. He had enlisted under Col. Stand Watie of the first Cherokee Regiment, known as the Cherokee Mounted Rifles, and was soon made lieutenant. Later, when he and Mary's brother John came home on furlough, Clem was wearing a captain's chevrons on his sleeve.

While Clem was fighting, Mary Rogers and the other Schrimsher women decided to flee to Texas for safety. With incredible difficulty they made this long journey, and arrived at last at Bonham, Texas. There, in a frame house on Bois de'Arc Creek, they lived for the duration of the war.

It took courage to sing and joke and tell gay stories to cheer the downhearted during those dark months, but Mary managed it, somehow, in the midst of plowing and planting and other hard work which she shared with the rest of the women.

When at last the war was over, Clem Rogers was without either money or a job. The Indian Territory was a devastated region. Farms were over-run with weeds, houses were burned, cattle and horses driven off. But this young American who had fought for a losing cause, was not discouraged. He rented a small house for Mary and their new baby daughter, hired a Cherokee boy to look after them, and went to work driving mule teams to a freight wagon all over the southwest. He was grateful for the opportunity to make even small wages, and soon he was beginning to save money. Then he decided to go back to the Cooweescoowee country and again start in business for himself. When he was able, he acquired a small piece of land on the Verdigris river, and began farming and raising cattle.

It was beginning all over again for him and Mary, but they were not afraid, and once more they set to work to make a real prairie home. They prospered, and in 1875 Clem built a double log house, plastered on the inside and shingled and weatherboarded on the outside—the finest ranch house in the district.

During the years six children had been born to Clem and Mary, and of those four were living when, two years after the new house was finished, on November fourth, 1879, Will Rogers was born.

Chapter 2
EARLY DAYS ON RAB'S CREEK

WILLIAM PENN ADAIR ROGERS, seventh and last of the Rogers children, was named for his father's good friend William Penn Adair, the brilliant Cherokee soldier and statesman. This long and impressive name was promptly shortened however, and for the first few years of his life he was known to his family and friends as "Willie."

He was a blue-eyed, sandy-haired boy, full of life and fun, and he grew like any normal healthy colt on his father's range. He was devoted to his mother, but his hero was his older brother, Bob, who rode a little flea-bitten pony named Kaiser, and whenever Bob and Kaiser were around, Will had eyes for no one else.

The Rogers household was a busy one. Clem Rogers worked early and late on his farm. He was raising cattle, hogs and horses at a profit, and his land produced so much wheat that sometimes there would be as many as fourteen binders working at one time in his wheat fields. At the time of Will's birth Clem was not only a successful farmer and stockman, but

WILL'S MOTHER, MARY AMERICA ROGERS
(Courtesy Will Rogers Memorial and Birthplace)

had begun to be a figure in Cherokee politics, and was serving the   first of his five terms in the Cherokee senate from the Cooweescoowee district.

Inside the ranch house Mary Rogers and the Negro women who helped her, were equally busy, for there were five active youngsters to clothe, feed and look after, besides the countless household tasks that must be done each day. This was no small undertaking for a woman in a frontier home, but Mary did it well. And she not only managed her own household capably, but she never was too busy to be of service to any neighbor who might need her.

Mary and Clem were the very soul of hospitality, and the Rogers house was seldom without visitors. It was Mary's custom to bring some family home from church with her for dinner each Sunday—and in those days when people came for dinner they stayed all day and often all night as well. Mary always fed them bountifully, kept them as long as they would stay, and when they departed, they did not go away empty-handed. Perhaps it was apples or peaches from the orchard, a basket of grapes, or a bit of Mary's own baking that her guests took home with them. But it was always something.

Clem often invited neighbors to go fishing with him, and when he did, these neighbors would come the night before so that a good early start could be made. Whole families would go in wagons to Four Mile Creek, where the perch and bass were so thick that they would strike not only at the baited hook, but also at the colored cork on each line. The catch would always be taken back to the Rogers farm where a big fish dinner would be served.

An atmosphere of such friendliness could not fail to leave its impress on the child, Will Rogers, and it implanted in him an open-hearted generosity that was one of his chief characteristics throughout his life.

Will's early years were much like those of other children in ranch houses or on farms. He rarely went to town because there were no towns near. Vinita, thirty miles east, was a straggling Indian village on the prairie, Old Claremore was a tiny cluster of stores on the stage route from Vinita to Albuquerque, and Tulsa was then only a switch. But Will was not interested in towns, and cared only for ranch life. There were so many fascinating things to do on his father's farm that the days were not long enough to get them all done.

Among the most exciting events in those days were the terrible but beautiful prairie fires that sometimes swept the Territory in fall and winter. A careless pipe-smoker or some hunter would often be responsible for these devastating fires. But no matter what caused it, a prairie fire could be a thing of terror. If it got well started, no creeks could stop it, and it would come roaring over the prairie at a fearful pace. It moved so swiftly that often the fastest horse could not outrun it.

MOSE TIES HIS COAT OVER HIS HORSE'S HEAD AND STARTS A
COUNTER FIRE

When a blaze was sighted dangerously near his stack yards, Clem Rogers and his farm hands would quickly load sacks and barrels of water and rush out on the prairie to fight it while from an upstairs porch of the Rogers' house, the frightened women and children would watch it with awe.

Despite its destructiveness, a prairie fire at night was a gorgeous sight. A dull red glow would first appear on the horizon, disclosing magnificent billows of thick smoke boiling up angrily. If the wind was strong the smoke would be black and roll low along the ground. But if there was little or no wind, its white billows would tower high in the sky, the curve of each fold dyed with a scarlet luster.

Sometimes the blaze would be so close that it could be heard at the Rogers' house, crackling and popping like a thousand giant whips, the leaping tongues of flame hurtling down-wind, hungrily licking the grass from the prairie. And sometimes the men themselves had narrow escapes from death.

At one time Mose Walker, a black cowboy working for Clem Rogers, got caught on the prairie with a fire sweeping down upon him, and no shelter near. But Mose did not run. Although he knew he could not get away from it, he kept his head. Quickly he lit a small counter fire of his own, so that he could follow along in the clear spot it burned ahead of him. With little time to waste, he leaped from his horse, threw his coat over the animal's head, pulled over his own head the knotted bandana he wore around his neck, and held on to the reins with all his strength. The roaring inferno swept over man and horse, but the little path Mose had burned split the flame and save for minor scorchings, Mose and his horse made a clean escape.

Many times as a child Will Rogers saw the magnificent spectacle of a prairie fire and watched with mingled alarm and excitement as his father and the men went out to fight it.

A much less dangerous but equally exciting experience was his too, in those early days of his life. There came a time when he was taken out to the wheat fields to ride old Lummox, the lead horse of one of the Rogers' binders. Lummox was a big, gentle gray, and Mose Walker, foreman of the crew, placed a small saddle on Lummox's back and lifted Will into it. Small boy though he was, Will stuck on well, and rode for hours, laughing and shouting at the top of his lungs.

From that time on there was nothing he liked so well as riding old Lummox, and for the rest of his life Will Rogers never was happier than when he was on a horse.

Now, Rab Rogers, Clem's former slave, had settled on a creek seven miles west of the Rogers' place. It was the spot where Clem's old homestead and trading post had been before the war, and Clem had given it to Rab because he liked him and knew he was a good farmer, honest and industrious.

Rab, as was the custom with the slaves, had taken his master's name, and though he was now free and no longer bound to Clem, there was a perfect understanding between the two men. When Rab needed horses, a cow, or a piece of machinery, Clem Rogers gave them to him. And when Clem needed extra hands to help him on the farm, he borrowed one or more of Rab's sons.

Rab Rogers was an unusual Negro. He weighed two hundred and sixty-five pounds, wore his hair down to his shoulders like an Indian, and although he never had seen the inside of a school house, he was considered the smartest Negro in the country, and was looked up to by the other black people in the neighborhood.

Six sons: Nick, Jack, Houston, Clem, Jasper and Ike, had been born to Rab and his wife, Rody; also five girls: Clara, Rose, Lucy, Grace and Margaret. Will Rogers knew all these children well and played at their house almost as much as he did at his own.

When he was no more than six years old, he would be taken over to Rab's house for a day's visit, and in the evening Clem and Mary would drive over and bring him home. Usually it was not easy to persuade the boy to leave this group of jolly playmates.

"Ready to go home, Will?" Clem would ask him.

"No, Papa," Will would answer, "I'll come home next Sunday. Jack and Hous will bring me home."

Clem would laugh heartily at this, and though Will eventually would be persuaded to leave, it was not without a struggle. Friendships such as this were a bit unusual in that day and time, but there were few white children in Will's neighborhood, and these children enjoyed each other's company.

Rab's house was a rambling, two-story frame dwelling of seven rooms, and stood by a creek in a grove of black locust trees in the heart of the wild Cooweescoowee district. The family got water from a cool spring that splashed down from over-hanging rocks, about fifty yards from the house. A big barn, large enough to hold a world of hay, and with stalls enough to accommodate sixteen head of horses, was nearby.

It was an ideal place for a little boy to play, and Aunt Rody was a fine cook. Supper would be served about dark in the fire-lit kitchen, and after a long day of climbing trees and romping about the pastures and in the woods, Will Rogers would attack with savage appetite the ham, prairie chicken, quail, hot biscuits, sweet corn, thick milk gravy and apple butter that

Aunt Rody served.

But it was not only at meal times that these healthy young boys ate. It seemed they were always eating. Often they would climb up into Rab's wild cherry trees and eat the black cherries, or they would wander down into the shady creek bottoms to find the yellow May-apples and, later, the paw-paws, persimmons and black haws that grew there, rank and thick, in the autumn. The Negro boys taught Will to locate the paw-paws by smell, and he soon became as proficient at this as they were.

There were few blacks in the Cherokee country who could tell ghost stories as well as Rab Rogers. Naturally a good talker, Rab gave his yarns a flavor of sincerity because he believed most of them himself.

After supper on the days when Will Rogers visited at Rab's, the little boys would gather round and listen, wide-eyed, to the tales Rab told while waiting for Will's father to come and take him home. The woods that ran right to Rab's back door were dark and full of weird night sounds. Wild cats squalled, the tufted owl gave his hollow, eerie cry, and lightning bugs veined the darkness in slow phosphorescent flight. All these things lent just the right atmosphere for Rab's stories.

"Now doan you boys forget," the man would say at the end of his story, "if you're evah travelin' along and see a ghost or a sperit, doan nevah shoot it, or try to fight it, or it'll kill you!"

The little boys would shiver, glance out at the darkness beyond the lighted room, and beg for more stories.

The ghost story that Rab told oftenest was about old Bender. Several years earlier, a white man had come one day to Rab's house. He was surly, wore rough clothes and boots, and said his name was Bender, and that he had been a scout in the war. He had a shot-sack full of gold and silver coins, and carried them with him all the time. He told Rab he had robbed and killed people for them, and Rab believed him. Bender didn't sleep in Rab's houe, but stayed out in the smoke house and kept his horse—a bald-faced bay—saddled all the time and hidden nearby.

One day old Bender took sick and died soon after. The Indians came and buried him about a mile and a half from Rab's house. No one ever found the shot-sack full of coins, but Rab and his boys looked hard and long. Rab kept the outlaw's horse and named it "Bender" after the suspicious-looking man who had been its owner.

After a while everyone forgot the man, so Rab's story went. But about five months later, old Jonas Ragswell, a Negro who lived down by the ford, came home one night scared almost white, and told a story that rang up and down the creek for many a day.

He had been hunting cattle, he said, and as he passed within a few yards of where old Bender was buried, he felt a touch on his leg that sent the cold chills over him. Looking down, he saw to his horror, Bender the outlaw, his face fiendish in the twilight, grasping at the stirrup and the saddle horn in an effort to mount the horse. Old Jonas let out a strangled yell, the horse began bucking, and when he finally got it under control, a quarter of a mile down the road, the apparition was gone. The frightened man then ran the horse every step of the way home.

"Well," Rab would say, "about three weeks later I was comin' home late from plowin' and I seed old Bender's ghost too. I was walkin'—drivin' ole Dan and Helen ahead of me —and when I passed the place where the Indians had burried Bender, his sperit ran up and tried to take the lines away from me."

"What'd you do?" Will Rogers would ask excitedly.

"What'd I do?" Rab would exclaim. "Why, I jest let him have them ole lines and I started leggin' it for home. The horses was skeered too; they know when a sperit's aroun'. They run, jes lak I did, and when they passed me, down by the dugout, I grabbed the lines as they went by and come on home with 'em."

The story of Bender was one that the little boys

never tired of hearing. They talked about it among themselves, and wondered what they would do if "ole Bender's sperit" chased them. And then one day they found out.

The two black boys, Clem and Jasper, had driven over to Clem Roger's place in the two-horse hack, to get some apples, and Will was returning with them. They had stopped to go swimming in the creek, and darkness overtook them before they could reach Rab's house. The sun went down behind red clouds, the prairie lay in deep shadow, and bull bats dove from above the trees.

The three boys were more than a little frightened, for they must pass within a few yards of where old Bender was buried; the creek prevented their taking any other route home.

Clem, the oldest, was driving. The horses were swinging along with a pleasant clatter of hoofs, and the wheels sang in the dust.

Suddenly Jasper let out a shriek. "Yondah's old Bender!"

"Where? Where?" shouted Will and Clem.

"Right theah!" screamed Jasper. "Cain't you see him?"

"I see him! I see him!" shouted Will, peering through the dusk. "Don't let him jump in the wagon!"

Jasper did not wait, but dived under the wagon

sheet and Will instantly followed him, while Clem
began whipping the horses. Clem had not seen the
outlaw's ghost, but he was taking no chances, and
poured the whip to the faithful team. They were three
frightened boys when finally they reached Rab's house
and told their story.

"I tole you! I tole you!" Rab said. "He tried to jump
in the buggy with me about a week ago and I had to
beat him off with the whip!"

"But what if you ain't botherin' him?" asked Willie
Rogers, big-eyed and panting.

"He gits chillern anyhow!" said Rab. "Chillern's
what he wants!"

Clem Rogers rode over on horseback a little later
that night to take Will home, and as he lifted the boy
into the saddle, Will said:

"Papa, we'd better go around by Uncle Hous'es or
old Bender'll run us!"

"Well I'm goin' that way," Clem Rogers promised,
as though grateful for the warning.

Behind them in the yellow rectangle of Rab's doorway the anxious blacks stood and watched them until
they rode from view behind the dark blur of trees.

Chapter 3
FIRST SCHOOL DAYS

ONE OF Clem Rogers's best cowboys was a black fellow named Dan Walker, whom Clem had brought from Fort Gibson. Dan was the best roper on the ranch. He could rope a cow any way you asked him to. He could get her by the horns, or around the neck, or by any one of her four feet. He was also a top bronco rider.

One day he rode over to Rab's creek and married Agnes, the daughter of Houston Rogers. Agnes was the best-liked colored girl on the creek. She was kind, sympathetic, a hard worker, and a good cook. She and Dan settled first on the McClellan place, but some years later they moved to "the ranch," a rough, three-room frame house that Clem Rogers had built near his cattle pens, about three miles over the hill from the Rogers home.

Since this was much nearer than Rab's place, Will Rogers soon spent a great deal of time with Dan and "Aunt Babe," as Agnes was called. Dan and Babe had four boys by now, and a tom-boy girl named Charlotte; and all of them were favorites with Will. He and

Charlotte would drive Aunt Babe almost crazy with their noisy games, but Will would stop playing with Charlotte any time to be with Dan Walker. He admired Dan enormously because he was a good roper and rider, and because Dan was teaching him to ride a pony.

Next to riding, the sport that Will enjoyed most at Dan's was the all-day fishing trips to "perch hole" on the Four Mile branch, with Charlotte and her brother Bud, and Anderson Rogers, Houston's son. They would cut hickory poles with their pocket knives, use straight sticks for corks, and bent needles for hooks. They would heat the needles in the fire and bend them into hooks, tying string in the eye. They used grasshoppers for bait. Charlotte was allowed to pack this bait in a can and carry it, and later, to cook the fish the boys caught.

Will was the best fisherman of them all. "I'm gettin' a bite," he would whisper, and pretty soon he would pull out a perch. If he found a particularly good fishing hole, he would have the others come over and fish with him. "Put your hooks down here, 'side of me," he would say generously.

Sometimes they found a little backwater hole, and when they did, they knew just what to do. They would take a sack, put a stick across the mouth of it to keep it spread, and hickory bark down the sides to draw it

ALL-DAY FISHING TRIPS TO THE "PERCH HOLE"

along with. Then they would seine and pull in perch, mudcats, crawdads, red haws and suckers.

While the boys lay comfortably in the shade talking, the faithful Charlotte would clean the fish and cook them. The fire was built in a hole the boys had dug in the ground. When the fire burned down low enough, Charlotte would put little green twigs across it and lay the fish on these twigs. Aunt Babe always gave them salt and bread and butter before they started out.

Of all the days to visit at Dan's, Saturday was the best day of all, Will thought, for then several black children usually came in to spend the day and there was plenty of fun and excitement. One of the favorite amusements at that time was to bend down a little sapling and pretend it was a bucking horse. Will would sit astride the bent sapling, pull his hat down tight, and call out: "All right, boys, turn him loose!" The other boys would loose their hold on the sapling, throwing up their arms as cowboys did when they turned a bronco loose. Will would then buck up and down on the sapling, fanning it with his hat and yelling as he had heard Dan Walker yell when he was riding a particularly bad bronco.

Once in a while the sapling proved too strong for Will and he would be thrown off. He would roll over and over on the ground while the others yelled with laughter; but he always got up, brushed himself off, and grinned. "Whoopee!" he would yell, "that sho' was a bad 'un, wasn't it?"

Will Rogers was also a boy who liked to tease. It wasn't malicious teasing, just thoughtless tormenting, for like any other boy he liked to have a good time, and have it often.

Ike Rogers, one of Rab's youngsters, who came over to play in those days, thought the world of Will and would obediently do anything he asked. One day Will took advantage of this and gave Ike a bad scare. Two large, beautiful peacocks were at the Rogers farm and all the little Negroes lived in mortal dread of the male, a splendid bird that was fond of strutting and pruning his feathers. Once Will secretly coaxed the peacock into the barn and shut the door. Then he hunted up Ike.

"Ike, go out in the barn and get my rope," he ordered, and Ike obediently toddled on his errand, went into the barn, closed the door behind him and groped around in the half light for the rope. Then, to his horror, he saw the peacock. It began to swell up and spit at him, and Ike started bawling and knocking all the harness down trying to get out of there. When he finally made it and burst from the doorway, Will Rogers rolled on the grass, roaring with laughter.

But in spite of his love for teasing, Will was a general favorite with his playmates, not only because of his good nature and love of fun, but because he was so generous. He always shared everything he had with others, and never was known to do a mean or selfish act. Sometimes he got into scrapes through high spirits and thoughtlessness, but he always acknowledged his fault frankly, and was so sorry for what he had done, that everyone forgave him at once.

In his generosity and unselfishness he was like his parents who were always doing something for others, and never minded how much trouble it was. Mary constantly visited the sick and needy, taking them medicine, food and clothing. And Clem gave freely not only of his money to people who were in need, but he helped them in other ways as well.

An illustration of his kindness is an incident that once happened, causing much excitement and consternation for a time. There was in that country a half-breed named Bud Trainor. He was a mean, insolent fellow who would empty his six-shooter at a Negro's feet just to see him jump, and would shoot their dogs and chickens for sheer deviltry. One night at a colored dance, Bud Trainor got into an altercation with two of the Rogers boys. At once he pulled his gun, fired at Jasper, and, missing him, fired point blank at Jasper's brother Jack. His aim was bad and he missed Jack also, but so narrowly that Jack's face was powder-burned. There is no knowing what would have happened next, but Nick Rogers, seeing his two brothers in danger, stepped out from behind a door and shot Bud Trainor through the head.

Sheriff Ward of Claremore rode out to Rab's creek and took the colored Rogers boys to the United States Court at Fort Smith. It was no joke in those days to have to face Judge Isaac C. Parker, the famous "Hanging Judge," whose court was known as "The Gates of Hell." Judge Parker was perfectly fair, but he was stern. In his hands the law became a fearful avenger.

The colored Rogers womenfolks wept piteously when the boys were taken away, for they never expected to see them alive again. But when Clem Rogers heard what had happened, he sent a messenger with a letter to Judge Parker explaining the details of the killing, and in three days the Rogers boys were back home. The judge had freed them without trial, on the word of Clem Rogers. The incident shows Clem's standing in the old Cherokee Nation.

Those were stirring times out on that wild frontier— rough, dangerous times in many ways. But to young Will Rogers, growing up on his father's range, that frontier was the garden spot of the world. He had a comfortable home, kind parents, jolly playmates, and the whole country-side for a playground. But above all, he was happy because he was learning to rope and ride, the two things he cared for most in all the world.

However, Mary Rogers felt that fine though this might be, there were other things her boy must have if he were to enjoy an equal chance with other boys in the business of facing life, and that one of these was an education. And one morning in 1887 she spoke her thoughts to Clem.

Clem Rogers paused on his way to the field and stood by the fireplace thoughtfully kicking the smoldering chunks of wood.

"That's right, Mary," he said at last, "but where can we send him?"

Sending children to school on the frontier was a problem. The Indian Territory was not then a state, and the United States government maintained no schools there. There was a school at Oowala, a few miles from the Rogers home, but it lay across the river, and high water often prevented people from crossing.

At last it was decided to send Will—who was now seven years old—to the newly-erected Drumgoole school, three miles southwest of the town of Chelsea, then only a store and a depot on the prairie. This school was one of a chain of neighborhood schools that the Cherokees had built all over the Nation. For fifty years the Cherokee people had set aside a portion of their national fund to maintain schools and furnish books. These schools were used for church purposes as well.

Since the Drumgoole school was located twelve miles from the Rogers home, it was arranged for Will to stay with his sister, Sallie, who had married Tom McSpadden, a young stock farmer, and lived on a ranch about three miles from the school.

Each day Will rode his pony to and from school, and each day Sallie would put up his dinner in a little leather box. This box Will hung on the saddle horn of the new shop-made saddle that Clem had bought for him.

The Drumgoole school stood in a pretty little grove of locust trees on Little Coal creek, and was a one-room cabin made of post oak logs, daubed and chinked. It had a plank floor and a gable roof of home-made clapboards. The children sat on rough puncheon benches made of split logs dressed down and smoothed with a broad ax, and with thick wooden pegs for legs. These crude benches had no backs at all for the children to lean against.

The school was principally for the children of full-blood or mixed-blood Indians on the tribal roll, although a white child might attend if its parents paid a tuition fee of one dollar a month. Most of the full-blood Indian children came of poor families. The girls wore calico or gingham dresses, high shoes, and had their hair braided down their backs and tied with red ribbon. The boys wore home-made jeans and shirts, and sometimes overalls.

Will got along very well in his first school. He learned his lessons without having to study a great deal. In fact, he learned so easily that he spent much time looking out of the schoolroom window. At first his teacher thought this was just idle staring, but she was wrong. Will's eyes were fastened admiringly on a new tan saddle on the back of a schoolmate's pony, tied to a tree just outside the schoolhouse. This saddle had big fur pockets that hung down on each side, it creaked gloriously and was a newer saddle than Will's—so new that when the wind was just right, the boy could smell the new leather. He spent many an hour looking longingly at this saddle.

The teacher, Miss McCoy, a small, dark-haired girl with Cherokee blood in her veins, had been educated at the Cherokee Female Seminary at Tahlequah. She managed to keep a pretty fair order among her pupils without doing much whipping. Her method of punishment was to keep pupils in at recess or stand them up on a desk in front of the school with their faces to the wall. Her principal problem was with the full-blood children, most of whom spoke only a little broken English, though they were proficient in Cherokee.

The little full-blood boys were rough and clannish,

with peculiar notions of how to play at recess. If one of them got to wrestling with a white or mixed-blood boy, the other full-bloods would jump in and help their companion. They did not always know when to stop. Once when a half-breed boy named Jack Cochran was wrestling with one of them, three others leaped on his back, pushed him down in a gopher hole and were filling his eyes and mouth with double handfuls of dirt, when one of the larger boys discovered them and rescued poor Jack.

Will Rogers, one of the youngest pupils in the school, was known as a quiet boy. He kept well in the background during the arguments and fights that took place during recess, and never spoke until he was sure of what he was going to say.

But though he did not say very much, he was an observant boy. If any of the children came to school in old shoes or ragged clothes, Will, deeply touched by this evidence of poverty, would tell his mother about it the next time he saw her, and Mary Rogers would see that other clothes were provided. Once, at Will's suggestion, she sent Miss McCoy enough calico to provide dresses for twelve little girls in the Drumgoole school. Young as he was, Will Rogers always looked out for his less fortunate schoolmates, and often divided the contents of his well-filled dinner box with those who had only scantily filled pails.

Occasionally the school would put on a little program, and at such times Clem and Mary Rogers
would drive over to see it. One of Will Rogers's first
public appearances was on such a school program,
when he wore a pasteboard star covered with silver
paper and proudly recited a verse beginning: "I am a
little star."

Will's new pony, a little chestnut mare, was the
pride of his life in those days. When school was over
he could scarcely wait to mount her and gallop off
toward Sallie's house. But sometimes when the
weather was cold and the little mare had stood saddled
all afternoon, she would rear and frisk so much that
the teacher would make Will dismount and wait,
much to his chagrin, while one of the older boys rode
her several times around the schoolhouse, to warm
her up a bit.

Will went only one term to Drumgoole, and a few
years later the little school closed its doors forever,
when other schools were founded in Chelsea and at
other points. Later, when he was a man, Will Rogers
spoke of that first school of his that had, as he said,
"gone out of business" so soon after he left it. "Now,"
he said, "the weeds is higher than the school house
ever was."

And he was right. The old school building was torn
down long ago, and now weeds and cane grow high

about the spot where it once stood. It is a desolate and lonely place, with nothing much to mark it any more save a forest of tiny locusts—shoots from the old trees that grew there when the boy, Will Rogers, went to school.

Chapter 4
HARD LESSONS

THE FIRST time Will Rogers saw Dan Walker throw a rope he was fascinated. Dan was seldom without his rope. He used it to catch his horse in the morning, he used it as a bull whip to hurry lagging cattle, and as a tow line to pull mired cattle out of bog holes or quicksand. He even used it to snake wood to the ranch house for Aunt Babe's kitchen stove.

But best of all, Will liked to see Dan throw his rope, and would stand for hours watching him.

One day Dan made a loop in his rope and laid it on the ground. "Heah, you Mack an' Will an' Charlotte!" he called. "Come ovah heah, I wanta show you how to rope."

They came on the run, eager to learn, and Dan chuckled at their clumsiness as he taught them to make the knotted honda, build a noose and shake it out in preparation for a throw. The children learned quickly. Will watched every move Dan made and tried to imitate him. He noticed that Dan didn't whirl his loop around his head before throwing it as many of the hands did, but spread it out at his side, and then flipped it forward at the target with a quick, sure toss.

Dan worked with the children tirelessly. At first he would fix the rope and lay it on the ground and make them pick it up to throw it. If they didn't do it right, he would scold them.

"Heah now," he would say, 'at's no way to throw 'at rope! I want you to do it right. Watch, an' I'll show you."

In Dan's big black hands the rope seemed almost human in its obedience. If Dan wanted the front foot of a horse, his rope went out and got it for him, neat and quick. If he wanted the top of a snubbing post, the loop sprang out of its coil, and reaching lazily and gracefully across twenty feet of ground, thwacked against the post with its back arc.

After Dan went to the field, Will and Mack and Charlotte practiced roping Dan's goats. Soon they were roping so well that the goats quit running and became so gentle that roping them ceased to be sport. Then Will and Mack began riding them. One of them would rope a goat by the horns, snub her to the fence, milk her, then hold her while the other clambered on, dug his fists deep into her wool, and hugged his legs around her tight. The goats soon learned that they could knock the boys off by running into a rail fence. Will and Mack would laugh when they fell off, but sometimes their laughter would be cut short when the angry goat turned on them with lowered horns. Then they would have to run and jump through the fence, or, if there wasn't time for that, roll under it.

Will was always glad when spring came and grass began to grow on the prairie, for that meant that the cattle would be turned out to pasture, and there would be plenty of roping and riding at the ranch.

Dan forbade the boys to rope or ride the calves, but after Dan left for the field, Will would go and beg Aunt Babe to let them do a little roping, and he would look at her so beseechingly that almost always Aunt Babe gave her consent, after warning them to be careful. With loud whoops they would spring for the cow lot.

One morning Clem Rogers made Will and Mack supremely happy by taking them to the branding pen with him and letting them help him and Dan with the calf branding. It was the boys' job to rope the calves from the ground, so they could be dragged up to the fire where Clem earmarked them with a knife, and big Dan wielded the branding iron.

This was a thrill the boys never forgot. They were right in the midst of everything—the heat, dust, profanity, the acrid smell of sweating men and horses, the bawling of the terrified calves, as Dan's branding iron was pressed to each animal's heaving side. But the boys worked well. They caught the calves any way they could—sometimes around the neck, sometimes around the belly. But they roped forty-six head that first day, and when night came, they were so tired and their arms so sore, that they could scarcely wait to tumble into bed.

Clem Rogers was doing a wise thing in giving Will a taste of hard work, and giving it to him early. And Will loved it. Roping and riding were forever in his thoughts. They became his chief interest in life, and the aroma of the cow country seemed to cling to him like hickory flavor to good barbecue meat, and to be reflected in his actions, writings, conversation, and everything he did.

"He even thought about ropin' calves in his sleep," Anderson Rogers used to tell of him. "Sometimes when mama worked ovah at the Rogah's house, me and Bud stayed all night there with her. Will's room wasn't fah from where we slept and we could heah him hollerin' an' flouncin' aroun' in his sleep. 'Catch him! Catch him!' he would yell, 'Rope him! Don't let him get away!' All the time he was sleepin' he was thinkin' about dem ole calves."

Rodeos were almost unknown in the Indian Territory in those days. But Will Rogers saw a great deal of bronco riding anyhow, though it wasn't done in an arena. And he learned a great deal about working cattle.

The rough life that this growing boy was leading was not without its casualties, as well as its instruction and fun. One morning Dan Walker came riding up to the Rogers house holding Will in the saddle in front of him, and carried the unconscious boy into the house.

Mary Rogers was badly frightened. "What happened, Dan?" she asked, her face pale with anxiety.

"His pony fell with him, Miz Rogers. It stepped in a wolf hole while he was runnin' a cow," Dan exclaimed as he laid the pale boy on the bed.

For a few days after that Will was pretty weak and wabbly on his legs, but soon he was as good as new and back in the saddle again.

And now his mother felt that he was not quite the same boy as formerly. Somehow he seemed older. Up to that time he had been just a happy, mischievous boy, always getting into things and needing to be watched and sometimes punished. But now he seemed to have grown wiry and stronger. Pulling goats and calves around at the end of a taut rope was developing his muscles. And sleep and fresh air, home-cooked food, and excitement were making him clear-brained and healthy. Will Rogers was growing up.

The next school he attended was the Harrell Institute, fifty miles away, at Muskogee, Indian Territory. This Institute was owned by the Board of Missions of the Methodist Episcopal Church South— Mary Rogers's own denomination.

The superintendent of the Institute was the Reverend Theodore Brewer who was considered a splendid school man. He and his wife were friends of Clem and Mary Rogers, and since May Rogers was already attending the Institute, they proposed that Will should be sent there also. Although there were a number of boys enrolled among the day pupils, only girls roomed and boarded at the Institute, but the Brewers made an exception in the case of Will Rogers and arranged for him to stay at the school, rooming with their young son, Bob Brewer.

Harrell Institute had a fine reputation and Clem and Mary Rogers were delighted that Will could have this exceptional educational advantage. But Will himself was not enthusiastic over it. He took almost no interest in his studies, and spent a great deal of his time in playing pranks on his fellow students.

His stay at Harrell Institute was a short one, for, when he went home at the end of his first term, he contracted measles, and, while he was convalescing from this illness, the first tragedy of his young life occurred.

Disease of one kind or another had raged all that spring at the Rogers home. Sallie and Maud had been seriously ill with typhoid fever, and Clem McSpadden, Sallie's four-year-old boy came down with measles and joined Will as a convalescent. Dr. Lane, the family doctor, made frequent visits to the invalids, but it was Mary Rogers who nursed and took care of them during that hard time.

And then one day Mary herself fell ill. For a time she struggled against this illness, but at last, being unable to shake it off, she was forced to take to her bed.

Dr. Lane was out of the country just at that time, so other doctors were called. But Mary grew worse day by day, and Clem, now greatly alarmed, wired Dr. Oliver Bagby of Vinita, to come immediately. He came as quickly as he could, driving the thirty-six miles across the prairie in four hours—excellent time for that day—but Mary Rogers was dying when he arrived, and at four o'clock the next morning she breathed her last.

Clem Rogers and his children were stunned by this sudden blow. It did not seem possible that those busy, capable hands were stilled; that the life of this well-loved woman was ended. Few people have meant more to their homes and communities than did Mary Rogers, and her death left a vacancy that could not be filled.

Will, then a lad of ten, was heart-broken, for he had

seen birds and animals die in the woods and knew
something of the permanency of death. He was only
just convalescing from his siege of measles and so
could not attend his mother's funeral, but stayed at
home with Aunt Gracey Greenleaf, an old colored
woman who had been cooking for the Rogers family
when Mary was taken ill. Aunt Gracey, her own eyes
wet with tears, soothed and comforted the little boy
as best she could.

It was a sad time for everyone. People for miles
around drove to the Rogers home to pay their last
tribute to Mary Rogers, and everyone, whether white,
black, or red, shed tears for this beloved woman who
had meant so much to them all.

Mary Schrimsher Rogers died without knowing of
the greatness her son would one day achieve, or
without realizing how importantly she had shaped
his character and personality by her wisdom and
tenderness during the first ten years of his life.

Forty years later Will Rogers said of her in a radio
broadcast on Mothers' Day:

"My own mother died when I was ten years old. My
folks have told me that what little humor I have,
comes from her. I can't remember her humor, but I
can remember her love and understanding of me."

Chapter 5
A HORSE AND A HERD

WILL ROGERS stood the death of his mother bravely. Sometimes when his playmates thoughtlessly mentioned her to him, he would burst into tears, but for the most part he controlled his feelings, and whatever sorrow he felt, he kept to himself.

Clem Rogers loved his children dearly, and now that Mary was gone, he did the best he could to be both father and mother to them. He knew how lonely Will, the baby of the family, felt, and one day he thought of something he could do for the boy—something he knew Will would like.

Colored Houston Rogers owned a buckskin pony named Comanche, a little square-made, cream-colored horse with faint black markings, standing fourteen hands high, and weighing only nine hundred and fifty pounds, and with no blemish on him save an open AR brand on his shoulder. Houston had raised this pony from a colt, had trained him carefully, and when Comanche was five years old, he started riding him over to the Rogers ranch whenever he went there to work for Clem.

Occasionally he would let the Rogers children ride Comanche, and soon they liked the pony so well that often when the day's work was done and Houston would go to the barn to get Comanche, he would find him gone. The children were riding him somewhere around the ranch!

Will was especially fond of Comanche, and Clem, seeing this, said to Houston one day: "What will you take for that hoss, Houston?"

"Sixty-five dollah," answered Houston.

"Will you swap him for that CM hoss yonder?"

"Yes, with ten dollahs to boot."

"Go put him in the barn, then," Clemn told him, and the colored boy, a little bewildered by the suddenness of the transaction, took the saddle off Comanche and put it on the CM horse, and Clem handed him a ten-dollar bill.

"I didn't exactly want to swap him off," Houston said later, "but Mistah Clem Rogahs kinda took me by surprise. I was out of work and needed a little extra spendin' money anyhow, so I let ole Comanche go."

Will was delighted at having Comanche for his own and grew very fond of the little buckskin pony. In fact, he said long after, that he never saw another horse he liked so well. Comanche was fast, intelligent, a good roping horse, and he hadn't a lazy bone in his wiry body. He was just the kind of horse a young boy might dream of owning, and from this time on, the two were together most of the time.

In those days Will was almost as fond of swimming as he was of riding, and he devised a way of combining these two pleasures very satisfactorily. He and "Doc" Payne, a white

WILL'S FATHER MAKES A SWAP FOR COMANCHE

boy about his own age, who worked for Clem Rogers, would drive five or six horses down to the Verdigris river, to a certain hole about fifteen or twenty feet deep, that was their favorite spot. The boys would take off their clothes and swim the horses back and forth across the river, one of them riding a horse and the other holding to the horse's tail. Will was utterly fearless, and often he would make "Doc" ride one of the horses out to where the hole was deepest and hold him there while Will used the horse's back as a diving board. This was such exciting fun that sometimes the boys even forgot to go home to dinner.

The summer days were not long enough for all the things that these boys found to do. They were together day and night, sleeping all over the ranch and racing their ponies on the prairie when they were not swimming in the Verdigris river.

But as autumn drew near, Clem Rogers began to think of putting Will into school again. After giving the matter some thought, he took the boy to the Presbyterian Mission School at Tahlequah, and enrolled him there.

Will liked this school no better than he had liked the others he had attended. The older he grew, the harder it was for him to be away from the ranch, and so at the end of the term he went back home.

The truth is that Will Rogers was not at all interested in getting an education. He was interested only in riding and roping, in teasing people and joking with them, in eating and having fun. The more serious things did not appeal to him at that age.

Curiously, there is a striking parallel here between Will Rogers and Mark Twain, the other great American humorist. Mark Twain hated school bitterly—worse even than Will Rogers did. In fact, he never went to school after he was eleven years old, and his mother, seeing he would never be reconciled to it, did not press him.

But Clem Rogers was insistent. He himself had grown up in the Cherokee nation where the splendid system of school was a tribal tradition, and in spite of the rough life he had led, he had obtained a good education for a boy of his time. Moreover, he knew how eager Mary Rogers had been that Will should get the best schooling possible, and he meant to carry out her wishes in this respect if he could. So once more he began to cast about in his mind for a new school for Will.

As time went by and nothing more was said about Will's education, the boy thought perhaps his father had given up all thought of sending him away to school again. He hoped this was true, for now, in addition to riding and practicing roping, another interest had come into Will's life—an absorbing interest to which he was giving much thought.

Some time before, Clem Rogers and two other men had gone to Fort Worth, Texas, and bought three thousand cows from Dr. Dan Taylor's ranch there. Spring is the natural time for cows to calve, and, as the Texas cows had been shipped up in the spring, a number of calves had got lost from their mothers in the confusion of shipping, and had never been claimed. Clem gave these motherless "dogie" calves—about eighty of them—to Will, as a beginning of a herd for the boy.

Usually these "dogie" calves, orphaned from their mothers at a tender age, have a difficult time, because they have no milk to drink. But Will Rogers worked hard to keep his "dogies" from starving. Often he would come home with a new calf across his saddle and would try to get one of the milk cows to let it suck. If this failed, he would teach it to drink from a pail. He took such care of these calves that soon he had them where they could look out for themselves, and turned them out on the prairie.

Clem was greatly pleased that Will took such interest in the orphaned herd, for, like most cowmen, he hoped his son would one day take charge of the entire Rogers herd.

"By Gad, Son," he said one morning, a gleam of fun in his eyes, "we must figure out a branding iron for you. We can't have your cattle and mine gettin' mixed up together, can we?"

"No suh, we sho' can't," Will said, frowning seriously as he had seen adults do when they wrestled with business problems.

That night Clem and Will got their heads together and figured out a branding iron for Will. They decided to use one of the andirons in the Rogers fire place. This andiron was a round O supported by what looked like the inverted crutch of a sling-shot and would be the very thing for Will's calves. The boy was delighted with this and when branding time came, Clem's men ran Will's calves into the pen and Will himself was allowed the thrilling experience of dabbing the hot iron on the flanks of his "dogies."

All this fired his interest in cattle until soon he could talk of little else. He would get up at dawn and lope Comanche out on the cool prairie to see how his little herd was coming on. It was great fun to ride at a dead run through the belly-deep blue stem that grew wild on the Rogers range, or just to pull up and listen to its steady ceaseless hissing as he watched it lean and double before a long flurry of wind, its surface changing and blending in blues and greens and yellows in the early morning sunshine.

But in spite of the new responsibility of his "dogies," Will had time for many other things. He owned a spotted greyhound named Jim, who could smell a coyote a quarter of a mile away, if the wind was right. Coyotes were thick on the prairies in those days, and often Jim would chase them all night long, with Will Rogers, the Bible boys, the Dawsons, and the Barkers hunting behind him. When they grew tired, they would build log fires and sleep on the ground. They hunted so much that soon they knew the bark of one another's dogs.

Bright Drake who lived just across the river, was another constant companion then. The principal sport of these two boys was roping coyotes from the back of a horse. They even tried roping wild turkeys, but soon found that the turkey could spread its wings and run for a short distance almost as fast as a horse. And even if they got close to it, the turkey would rise from the ground and fly.

So more and more they confined their attention to the coyotes. They thought there was no better sport in the world than to get a coyote out on a long smooth stretch of ground where he couldn't dodge into timber, and then give chase.

One day Bright's mother made some gingerbread and tea cakes, and packed a lunch which included several ribs of raw venison. The boys rode out on the prairie a mile or so, built a fire, and broiled their deer ribs on sharpened green sticks, over a bed of coals. After they had eaten their lunch, they mounted their ponies and galloped out to "jump" a coyote.

Soon they had flushed one and the chase was on. Yelling and laughing they took turns trying to rope the speeding animal. The coyote ran low, his ears laid back and his bushy tail floating behind him like a streamer. Time after time their loops settled over his gray shanks, but each time he would hump his tail and dodge or jump through their nooses before they could draw up on him.

As they rode pell-mell across the prairie they called to each other.

"I like to got him that time," Bright yelled, trying to coil his spend rope and keep an eye on the coyote too.

"I'm a gonna git him this time," Will shouted back, bending low over his saddle and cutting across the little wolf's path.

At last, with an especially adroit toss of his rope, Bright caught the coyote, and the boys led him back to the ranch, tied him up, and tried to make a pet of him. But the creature would not eat, and finally had to be killed by one of the cowboys.

Probably the most fun Bright Drake and Will Rogers had was accompanying Clem Rogers in the short cattle drives he occasionally made to Chelsea. On these trips Clem, Will, and a half dozen cow hands from the Rogers ranch would drive the herd—usually a bunch of five hundred steers—over to the Drake placed, arriving at night, just in time to bed down the herd on the Drake range, where they were allowed to rest a whole day.

Before sun-up on the second morning, the whole outfit would be on its way to the loading pens in Chelsea, eight miles distant.

It took all day to make the trip and noon would find them out on the prairie, only part way there. Then came the job that Will and Bright hated worst— watching the herd while the others ate dinner. Although the noon meal on such drives was rather meager, consisting usually of fried bacon, coffee brewed in a tin can, and some cold biscuits, it smelled mighty good to the two hungry boys who had helped drive cattle since daybreak.

"Gosh," Will would sigh, "I'll be glad when our turn comes. It's takin' 'em an awful long time to eat, ain't it?"

"Yeah," Bright would answer, "guess they've forgot about us bein' out here on herd."

When at last the stock pens were reached, it was the job of the two boys to help sort the cattle and drive them into the railroad cards. Usually it was hot, slow work, as the animals distrusted the elevated chute into which they must go. But eventually they would be loaded—twenty-five to each car—and the cowboys would slide the last car door shut and trail exhaustedly into Chelsea for supper.

If the loading were finished that night, the little party would ride back to the Drake ranch in the dark after supper, and, unincumbered by the herd, make fairly good time. On these nights Will Rogers would be a pretty tired boy and often would doze off in his saddle. But the faithful Comanche, without a touch of bridle or spur, would carry him safely and carefully.

Working cattle was a hot, dusty job with long hours and long, tedious rides, but young Will never complained. He was eager to learn all about it, for he was starting a herd of his own.

Chapter 6
AT WILLIE HALSELL COLLEGE

ALTHOUGH CLEM ROGERS was greatly pleased that Will was taking such interest in ranch life, he had by no means given up the idea of sending the boy to school again, and this time he chose the Willie Halsell college at Vinita, Oklahoma. This was a college owned by the Methodist Church South, and endowed by churchmen, townspeople and wealthy cattlemen. Here is the fall of 1892 Will Rogers reported to the registrar.

This was the fourth school he had entered and he looked about him curiously to see if it was different in any way from the others he had attended. It was a large school but, to Will, it looked and sounded and smelled like Harrell and the Presbyterian Mission. There was the same confining classrooms, each a snug, orderly, little prison, with desks and blackboards and only one door. The same hum of voices and peals of laughter as the old students greeted one another and their teachers after the summer vacation. There was the same schoolish odor of fresh chalk and oiled floors.

He looked out of one of the windows and his face

lighted up as he saw the greenish-brown sweep of prairie, and took a long whiff of the sweet air that blew into the room, stirring the window curtains. Will had never before realized how well he liked plain commonplace things such as grass and wind and horses and freedom. But with his mother's instinct for adaptability, he accepted his lot and once more attempted to fit himself to the peculiar routine of school.

Vinita was thirty-six miles from the Rogers farm and Will knew many of the students. He was assigned to a room with John McCracken and Charley Mehlin, two older boys, and Tom Lane, the son of Dr. Lane, a fine boy of about his own age. Their room was in the school building, a three-storied structure of brown brick trimmed with white stone, and was located on the outskirts of the town, just at the edge of the prairie.

Will enrolled in the preparatory department and, to his intense disgust, was required to take piano and oil painting in addition to the regular school course. His painting was not such a trial to him as he chose for his subjects chiefly horses and dogs. But his piano lessons he took as he would an unpleasant dose of medicine— with a wry face.

His piano teacher was Aunt Eugenia Thompson, and it must have required an amazing amount of patience on her part to take Will through his lesson period.

One morning when he had reported at Aunt Eugenia's house for his lesson, a group of his schoolmates came by and waited outside for him to finish his unpleasant task and walk to school with them. Presently Will appeared, looking crestfallen.

"You'd better jest go on and not wait for me," he told them, "I forgot to practice my piano lesson yesterday, and Aunt Eugenia says I've got to practice it this morning before I go to school."

His friends went on but had scarcely reached the railroad tracks a short distance away, when they heard Will's cheerful whistle in the distance.

"What about your music lessons?" they asked curiously when Will caught up with them. "How did you get out of it?"

"Oh," Will panted happily, "Aunt Eugenia kept pointin' her finger at the notes on the music page and sayin' 'What's that? What's that?' An' I said, 'That's yore finger, Aunt Eugenia.' Then she slapped me off the stool and told me to go on to school, and here I am."

In the room that Will and the three boys occupied, he and Tom were compelled to act as chore boys for the two older boys. Among their other duties they had to pull off the older boys' boots, and if they were too slow in doing it, they got themselves soundly thwacked with pillows.

Often, late at night, the two older boys would steal

down to the pantry in their bare feet to pilfer bread and butter and jelly. While they did this, it was the task of Will and Tom to stand guard, to put out the light and give the alarm if they heard anyone coming.

"What'd you get?" Will would whisper hoarsely when the boys came tiptoeing back to the room with their loot. And, because neither he nor Tom ever revealed these midnight raids on the pantry, they were always allowed to have their share of the spoils.

Although his roommate Tom Lane was a good student and got his lessons each day, his example did not inspire Will who seldom opened a book if he could help it. He had a good mind but disliked studying and was utterly indifferent to any but the subjects that appealed to him. When he wanted to he could scan a lesson quickly and make a good recitation, but he did not often care to do this. He had no interest at all in his grades and seldom bothered to look at his report cards. School, to him, was just something to be taken in his stride and got through with—like rope burn and saddle gall. It couldn't last forever, he knew.

Though he was far behind the other students in book learning, he had other learning that they did not possess. They were amazed at his knowledge of horses and cattle, and at the way he could talk about ranching and roping and branding. He knew by heart all the brands of the big ranches of the country, and most of the little ones too.

He brought Comanche back to school with him in his
second term and was fond of showing the boys what a
real cowboy was like. Joe Walker, who drove the stage
coach from Vinita to Southwest City, had nine sons,
one of whom, Charley, Will especially liked. Often Will
would ride over to Joe's house and give a one-man
exhibition of riding and roping for the Walker boys.
They would watch him breathlessly as he tore up and
down the road, roping the fence posts. When they
would run past him, at his invitation, and Will would
unerringly snare them around the neck with his rope,
they were greatly impressed with his skill and stood a
little in awe of him.

Although he was intensely masculine, Will rather
liked to play with girls at times. It is not improbable
that this was because he was an inveterate tease and
girls were easy prey for his pranks. He would walk
behind a group of girls on the way to school and,
singling out one of them, would say: "Well, I guess I'll
have to drive you to school this morning." And z—z-z-
i-p, his loop would drop neatly around the girl's arms.
The girls always submitted to this with the best grace
they could summon, for they knew very well that if
they remonstrated or got angry, it would only make
Will tease them the more.

Once when he had gone over to the other side of town

to Wooster college, the Congregational school, and had teased the girls there unmercifully, Chick Rogers, an Osage Indian girl, said when he left them: "I shouldn't wonder if we would hear from Will Rogers one of these days."

The other girls laughed heartily at that and who could blame them? What promise could Chick possibly see in a boy whose finger nails were always dirty, who rarely had his lessons, and who didn't care for anything but horses and cows and roping and teasing?

Chapter 7
THE WORLD'S FAIR AT CHICAGO

IN THE summer of 1893, a wonderful event happened in the life of Will Rogers. That was the year of the World's Fair at Chicago, and everyone was talking about what an exciting and amazing thing it was. The Indian Territory newspapers were filled with accounts of its splendor, and the railroads were offering special inducements to travelers. Interest in the Fair was at fever heat and everyone who had—or could borrow—the sum necessary for the trip, went to see this great exposition.

Clem Rogers, like many other stockmen that year, planned to ship a load of cattle to Chicago, timing the shipment with the date of the Fair, and when his arrangements were completed he told Will that he might go with him.

To thirteen-year-old Will, this was breath-taking news. He had seldom ridden on a cattle car and could scarcely believe it was true when, at last, he found himself in the caboose where he and his father were to stay during the trip, eating and sleeping with the train hands. It was a thrilling experience and he enjoyed it to the full, though now and then he felt a pang of unhappiness when he thought of the cattle packed so closely in their cars that they could not lie down no matter how weary they were.

But this was something that could not be helped, so he tried not to think of it and gave himself up to the enjoyment of the trip. It was fine, he thought, here in the caboose which was fitted up with a snug little office for the conductor and had long benches padded with black leather, built along the side for the crew and the passengers. He liked to feel the tremors from the distant engine as it took hold of the long string of cars and endeavored to move them, tremors that started with a faint clamor away up at the front of the train, and advanced rearward with rumbling reverberations that increased in shock until, suddenly, the caboose itself would leap and plunge in a final crashing jolt that would make the little kerosene wall lamps flicker and smoke, and the iron fire shovel that hung by the stove pound the coal box vigorously. He like to feel the heavy train slowly move and hear the bawling of the cattle in their dark prisons away up front, and the engine scream so faintly that he could scarcely realize it was pulling his train, and that he and Clem and the cattle were at last off for Chicago.

It was exhilarating that first night to climb the ladder to the rocking cupola in the top of the caboose, to sit there comfortably leaning back, watching the orange lights of the tiny towns crawl past and the winking stars overhead that always seemed to stay right with them. It was exhilarating too to listen to the wheels clattering noisily and to watch the engine's headlights up ahead, splitting the prairie darkness like a great illuminated eye.

He thought of Comanche with a fleeting pang of regret, and wished the little buckskin pony were going with him. He thought of his friends back home sleeping quietly in their beds, and felt sorry for them. Through the yellow square of light at his feet he could see the cowhands and the train crew amusing themselves on the caboose floor with draw poker, refreshing themselves from time to time with frontier whiskey. He tried to doze off but the strange movement, the noise and his own excitement forbade it, and at last Clem came and got him and showed him how to stretch out on the padded benches. Soon the game broke up, the clicking rails became less noticeable, the lamps were turned low, and the shadowy interior of the car became a gently swaying cube that blurred and faded in his sight.

At Chicago it was good to step down off the caboose and feel the ground under him, the cool lake breeze on his face; to stretch his cramped legs and look around at the swirl of people who thronged the horse cars on their way to the Fair.

Will Rogers never had seen so many people before nor heard such noise and confusion. Everyone was going to the Fair it seemed and, as soon as Clem had finished the details of his business, he and Will took a car and presently arrived at the Plaisance, a strip of land about a mile long and two blocks wide, through the middle of which ran a broad highway leading to the exhibits.

The Plaisance itself was a marvelous sight to the wide-eyed boy as he hurried along, holding tightly to his father's hand, their boots clopping and their spurs tinkling on the brick walks. On each side were restaurants, fountains, booths and shows, the like of which Will Rogers had never seen. Two streams of people moved through the Plaisance; one whose weary faces and tired gait showed that they had finished the Fair for the day; the other moving towards it with haste and eagerness, their guide books in their hands. Will and Clem moved with this latter group.

Their first stop was made to let Will mount and ride a great swaying camel—an unforgettable experience. Then other stops were made to taste, with exclamations of surprise, the marvelous foreign foods: Turkish and Hungarian dishes, oriental Johnny-cake, hot zelabiah in the Streets of Cairo, and the Arab's loaf which they broke and devoured with the help of a Bedouin in imitation of the hospitality of the desert.

At last they arrived at the Fair proper and for hours they looked at the exhibits that so lavishly and gorgeously depicted the life and craft of the nations of the world. But there was still more to come, and now Will was to have an experience more thrilling and wonderful than anything that had happened to him—a ride in the giant Ferris Wheel, first one ever built.

Everyone knew of this great wheel that reached almost three hundred feet into the air, with its thirty-six pendant coaches that could carry two thousand, two hundred and sixty people at a time. Will Rogers had heard of it, but scarcely believed what he had heard—it seemed too wonderful. And now he was to ride in it! Gingerly he stepped inside the car and took his seat, his heart beating fast with excitement. Presently the wheel began to move. Up-up-up went his car and Will, looking down, saw the ground slowly fall away from him. But when his car reached its top-most height and around him men were turning pale with fright and women were crying hysterically, the boy no longer looked but, clenching his teeth and closing his eyes, he instinctively dug his spurs into the wooden base of his seat.

His alarm lasted but a moment. Disciplining his fear, he opened his eyes and, from his perilous perch in the air, he looked down at the splendid view of the Fair buildings and saw the far-away gleam of the lake and, beyond it, the smoky mist that hid the city.

This boy, who later in his life was to travel so many thousands of miles in airplanes, got his first taste of air travel in the great Ferris Wheel at Chicago, and it was an experience he never forgot.

But Clem Rogers had saved the climax of the trip until the last, and one day he and Will went to see the famous Buffalo Bill Wild West show. Fresh from a four-year tour of Europe, this show had petitioned the Fair management for the right to play within the Fair grounds. This was refused them, the management holding that such a performance was undignified, so the Buffalo Bill Wild West show coolly rented a four-teen-acre site close to the main entrance of the Fair, and showed to six million people.

Will Rogers never in his life had seen anything like it, and his mouth dropped open in wonder and awe. He and Clem had box seats in the vast horseshoe amphitheater which accommodated twenty-two thousand people, and the acts were staged in the central arena which was open to the sky and not canvas-covered like the grandstand.

Never had this boy from the Indian Territory dreamed there could be such riding as he saw when, to the tune of lively music, the show's entire company of four hundred people came into the arena. Three were

the various Indian tribes, there were Arabs, Uhlans
from the Kaiser's crack Potsdam Reds, Russian Cossacks, French Chasseurs, British Hussars, Japanese
soldiers and American cavalry; and they dashed into
the arena as fast as their horses could run.

Then William F. Cody—Buffalo Bill himself—was
introduced and came thundering into the arena on his
big sorrel horse, Old Duke, the grandest parade horse
on earth. Majestically he swept off his big hat and in
a dramatic, far-reaching voice he shouted:

"Permit me to introduce the Congress of Rough
Riders of the World!"

For the next hour Will Rogers was conscious of
nothing but the gorgeous spectacle before him. Never
had he seen such horses, alert, beautifully groomed,
every nerve strained, and quivering with eagerness to
begin their act. And never had he seen such riders.

The first act was the Pony Express in which a man
on horseback with a mail pouch around his neck, rode
pell-mell, jumped off his horse and onto the back of
another. The instant he touched its saddle the fresh
horse jumped forward spiritedly, but the rider held on
tightly, pulled himself into the saddle and sprinted
once around the arena, halting at last to acknowledge
the deafening applause that greeted him.

Then other acts appeared. The Fifth Royal Irish
Lancers rode at full speed, lancing the paper hats off

each other. The French Chasseurs and Russian Cossacks rode brilliantly, as did the Arabs with their long draperies streaming out behind them as they tumbled off their mounts, climbed on again and formed themselves into pyramids of nine men, supported on the head, shoulders and knees of one brawny giant.

Act swiftly followed act until Will Rogers's head was swimming and he had forgotten everything in the world except the men and horses before him.

There was an Indian episode in which one hundred and fifty Sioux Indians participated. A midnight scene was depicted. Wild animals lay about in their lairs and night birds trilled in the trees. At sunrise, a brilliant lighting effect, there was a meeting of the tribes who executed a friendly dance. Then came a runner with warning of the approach of a hostile tribe. The attack was made with fearful vigor and the battle that ensued was a perfect picture of savage warfare.

There was another scene representing the prairie with a pond in the foreground to which wild buffalo came to slake their thirst. Then Buffalo Bill appeared, conducting an emigrant train of white people. In the gathering twilight they camped, lit fires, cooked and ate their supper and then gave a clever performance of a Virginia Reel on horseback. Meanwhile the arena was darkened, the camp sank into slumber and all was quiet. Presently a red glow appeared on the horizon. It broadened and deepened and soon the crackling flames could be heard, and the sleepy camp roused to the realization that the prairie was on fire.

The conflagration approached so near that soon the whole landscape seemed one lurid blaze, the roaring flames leaping down upon the foreground with wild fury. This scene was one of the grandest of the entire show and fairly bristled with excitement and thrills.

There was the reproduction of a prairie cyclone, there was the hold-up and robbery of the Deadwood Stage and even Custer's massacre, vividly presented with an enormous consumption of gunpowder.

Buffalo Bill himself gave an exhibition of rifle-shooting, and the best American cowboys obtainable did bronch riding that made Will crouch in his seat, squirming with excitement.

But the act that affected him most deeply of all, and was to inspire his whole career, was that of the Mexican vaqueros, the best ropers in the world. They rode out attired in gaudy costumes and riding at their head, dressed in embroidered jacket, buskskin trousers ornamented with brass buttons, a red sash, and a hat trimmed with gold braid, was the man who—old-timers still proclaim—was the greatest straight-roper of all time—Vincente Oropeza.

The Mexicans put on a fifteen minute act, roping running horses and their riders in every conceivable

VINCENTE OROPEZA, THE GREAT MEXICAN ROPER OF THE
BUFFALO BILL SHOW

way. Then, out in front, the great Oropeza began his roping and Will Rogers leaned forward with deadly concentration. The graceful Mexican did fluent spins, leaped lightly in and out of his whirling loop and snared the racing horse that was his foil, by its front feet, back feet, all four feet, the saddle horn and, finally, by its tail.

Oropeza's last stunt was to write his name in the air with his rope—one letter at a time. And when he did this to a thunder of handclapping, Will Rogers choked up, a mist was in his eyes, and in him was born a deep-rooted love for good roping that was to stay with him for the rest of his life.

Until that day Will Roger's roping had been the kind that every cowhand did on the ranch, catching a calf or steer or horse by neck or foot. But after seeing Oropeza, the boy was changed. All the way home he practiced roping every chance he got, spinning the noose and jumping in and out of it; and back once more at his father's ranch he worked at it harder than ever.

He had seen Oropeza—the greatest roper of all time. And from this time on, Will had a new goal always before him.

Chapter 8
BACK TO SCHOOL

AT THIS period of his life Will Rogers's favorite chum was Charley McClellan, a boy who lived across the Verdigris river, about five miles from the Rogers home. Charley was a bright, clean boy, very popular with all who knew him. He was one quarter Cherokee as was Will but, unlike Will, it was his greatest regret that he was not a full-blooded Indian. He would have like nothing better than to live in the open, roaming the plains and hunting wild buffalo on the prairie.

Although he as three-fourths white, Charley was so proud of his Cherokee ancestry and had such a desire to perpetuate the dress and customs of his tribe that he wore his scalplock in a long braid and in summer, when he and Will played around on their fathers' ranches, he went about with his face painted and his wiry body practically naked except for a breech clout, buckskin leggings and moccasins.

He had a way with Indians that Will envied. Once, when two train loads of Buffalo Bill's show, bound for Oklahoma City, stopped at Claremore to eat and feed their stock, everyone for miles around rode in to see them. Most of these show folk were friendly and talked and answered the questions that were asked them, but the proud Sioux Indians held themselves aloof and looked at the curious country folk as though they were so much dust under their moccasins. Charley McClellan paid no attention to their haughty manner but went fearlessly among them, and when they saw the braid of hair down his back and his authentic Indian costume, they grew so friendly that when the trains were ready to move on, they tried to persuade him to go along with them.

Another time Charley went to southwestern Oklahoma with his father on a business trip. His father, being detained longer than he had expected, gave his son the money to pay his fare and expenses and told him to go back home alone. While Charley was loafing about, waiting for the train to arrive, he chanced to see a group of Kaw Indians sitting in a blacksmith shop.

He went in at once, squatted down among them and tried to talk to them, but they were suspicious and refused to say a word to him. Carelessly, Charley let his shining braid of hair fall from under his hat and immediately the manner of the Indians changed.

"You Indian?" they asked him.

"Uumph," grunted Charley.

"What kind Indian?"

"Cherokee," Charley answered, beating his breast.

"Oh," they said in surprise, "Cherokees heap smart Indians!"

"Umph," admitted Charley.

The Kaws, wishing to capitalize on his wisdom, began at once to tell him something of their tribal affairs and to ask him for advice. Although the boy was only sixteen years old, he listened gravely and pursed out his lips as though giving the matter great thought.

"Keep your land," he said at last. "Don't sign any papers for white man." Not bad counsel, at that.

Meanwhile Charley had forgotton all about his train and, as it was now noon, he got to his feet and said: "You boys want something to eat?"

"Umph," the Kaws grunted eagerly.

That was enough for Charley. Taking them to a nearby restaurant the boy spent almost all his money feeding the hungry Indians. He had only enough left to take him as far as Sapulpa and there he got off the train and started walking down the railroad track toward home, carrying his grip.

Tom Smith, the conductor of a passing freight train, who had formerly worked for Charley's father, happened to see him and stopped the train and took the boy on home.

"Charley," his people scolded, "why in the world did you spend all your money on those Indians? You shouldn't have done it."

"They was hungry," Charley said simply and refused to say anything more.

Such incidents as these greatly impressed Will Rogers. He and Charley were together so much of the time that when Will went away to college he was unusually lonesome, and wrote to Charley urging him strongly to come to Vinita to school. At first Charley's parents would not agree to this, but after while, because Will begged so hard, it was decided that Charley should be allowed to attend Willie Halsell college.

Will was delighted. He was not going to mind so much being away from home if he could have Charley with him, and it was probably because of Charley McClellan that Will stayed for three years at Willie Halsell college—by far his longest stay at any school.

In one way these two boys were very different. Charley was a good student, took an interest in preparing his lessons and always had excellent grades, while Will took no interest at all in his studies and when called on to recite, would usually shift from one foot to the other, duck his head to one side and try to bluff his way through. But there was one thing that Will Rogers did faithfully and that was his roping practice. He always carried his rope about with him and would practice spinning it and stepping in and out of it as he had seen the great Oropeza do. He would have liked also to try Oropeza's stunt of catching a horse by any foot, but since no horse was available at Willie Halsell, he had to do his practicing on girls.

Aunt Laura Cooper who boarded and roomed about forty of the college boys in a big three-story house called The Annex, had a daughter Oneida, and it was she who was oftenest Will's rope victim. When she started off to school Will would walk behind her, ominously uncoiling his rope. Oneida well knew what was coming and, ashamed to be roped by the foot and thrown to the ground in front of a bunch of boys, she would threaten Will with every form of punishment she could think of. "I'll tell Mother on you," she would say, dragging the soles of her shoes along the pavement so that he could have no chance to get the rope under them. "I'll tell Professor Rowsey!"

But Will would only grin, and though poor Oneida would sometimes drag her feet an entire block, she would have to lift them when she came to a street intersection, and then—Ping!—Will's rope would go straight to the target, and down would go Oneida.

After Charley McClellan's arrival at school, he and Will began to go about to parties. At these little functions Charley would sometimes make speeches in Cherokee for the entertainment of the crowd, and Will would translate them, often inserting comical bits of his own that were not in Charley's speech. These

interpretations were among Will's earliest attempts at
entertainment and they were successful attempts, for
his audience was always in gales of laughter when he
had finished.

Other public appearances of Will's were the imita-
tions he gave on school programs. One of the best of
these was his imitation of a Negro preacher. For this
act he would blacken his face, put on white gloves, a
swallowtail coat and spectacles. Then he would begin
and as he warmed to his subject, he would stamp from
one side of the platform to the other, jump up and down
and pound the "pulpit," while the auditorium rocked
with laughter.

This faculty for arousing laughter by his quaint and
humorous sayings, was perhaps Will's greatest gift; a
gift he was to exercise more and more as the years
went by until, at last, he would come to be recognized
as one of the greatest humorists of this time. But
never, then or later, did his humor have a sting. It was
always kindly and genial.

From his earliest childhood Will Rogers had strongly
defined characteristics. He was by nature affectionate
and fun-loving and, though he loved to tease and play
pranks on his friends, there was no malice in him.
Underneath his love of fun and his careless ways,
there was a great sensitiveness which, in his early
years at least, sometimes caused him unhappiness.

But he was quick to forgive those who hurt him as he was to ask forgiveness when he himself was in the wrong, and this, as well as many other lovable traits, made Will Rogers a great favorite among his classmates at Willie Halsell.

During this second year at school he was still so careless about his personal appearance that sometimes Aunt Laura Cooper had to see to it that his face and hands and neck and ears were forcibly washed before he came to the table. This job of scrubbing fell to the lot of Oneida whose task it was to see that the boys, both big and little, were presentably clean at meal times, and while Will wriggled and squirmed and yelled as though he were being killed, she would do her work thoroughly, though she well knew that he would later take his revenge on her by roping her the next time he found an opportunity.

Although Will had plenty of spending money and could buy whatever clothes he wanted, he never seemed to care what he wore and always looked as though his clothes had been thrown on him. His hair was never in order but always hung down on his forehead, and his finger nails were far from immaculate. But he was so sunny, so open-hearted and generous, that no one could hold these minor delinquencies against him.

At the end of his second year at Willie Halsell—in the summer of 1894—Will went back to his father's ranch. Clem Rogers had recently married Mary Bibles, a good, industrious and religious woman who had been his housekeeper, and though she and Will got along well together, it was not to be expected that the boy would have the feeling for her that he had had for his own mother.

He was very happy to be at home again, leading the free, out-of-doors life that he liked so well, and he spent much of his time on Comanche, riding about the country visiting the friends he had not seen for so long, or riding out on the prairie to look after his herd of cattle. These little "dogies" had grown so fast that now many of them were ready to ship and this caused Will a good deal of pride and satisfaction.

But the summer was not without its mishaps, for one day Will broke his arm. It happened when he was roping steers and his rope, becoming tangled, crushed his arm against the saddle horn. This must have caused him much concern, for it was no slight thing to break an arm just when his roping was coming on so well. But whatever Will felt about this, he said nothing and continued to enjoy his months of freedom.

The summer passed quickly and all too soon the prairie was yellow with autumn flowers. And now the days grew shorter, the nights longer. Large flocks of teal and bluebill drifted own from the north and, along the banks of the Verdigris river, the thickets of dog-

wood, grape, persimmon and haws had already begun
to turn.

The happy carefree summer was ended and autumn
was here. This meant more schooling for Will Rogers
and, with a pang of regret that he must leave home

CHARLEY MC CLELLAN, WILL'S INSEPARABLE
COMPANION AT WILLIE HALSELL

when the prairie was at its prettiest, he packed his clothes and went back to Vinita.

Back again at college, Will found that most of his classmates had returned, and he went about greeting them all by the nicknames he had for them. Will always found appropriate nicknames for everyone; for Bert Oskinson it was "Wooley" which, in those days meant a farmer; "Puddin'" for Arthur Bynum whose favorite oath was "Aw puddin'"; and "Peach-Eater" for a boy named La Force who was unusually fond of peaches. Will himself did not escape being nicknamed and was called "Rabbit" because of his large ears, and sometimes even "Mule Ear."

Once more Will resigned himself to the routine of school days. Charley McClellan had returned to Willie Halsell and, as usual, the two boys were inseparable. But before a great while a change was noticed in Will Rogers—he was becoming more particular about his dress. He was as careless as ever about his studies, seldom looking at his books until he entered the class room and then trying to absorb the entire lesson in a few moments time in case he was called on to recite. But he was developing a pride in his appearance that was a new phase in his character.

In this third year at school it was no unusual thing to see Will wearing a flaming red necktie, fancy stitched boots and spurs—although he did not have his horse at school. And always he kept his pockets stuffed with chewing gum, which he handed out generously to everyone.

Charley McClellan became somewhat of a dandy too, and arrayed himself in clothes much like Will's and, before a great while, the two of them began to go about with the girls. Will, who only a short time before had made these same girls the victim of his whirling rope, now walked home with them after classes, proffering his gift of chewing gum.

He and Charley teased each other a good bit about their latest flames, but neither of them minded this. They were as fast friends as ever and Will's favorite pose was to stand leaning against Charley, his elbow on Charley's shoulder and his legs crossed so that everyone might get a good view of his fancy stitched boots.

But although Will was changing from a little boy into a sturdy young lad and although he was giving some thought now to the girls, his greatest interest still was riding and roping. Nothing else could crowd these things from his mind.

Just behind the school there was a one-hundred-and-sixty acre blue grass pasture, and Will and Charley and some of the other boys conceived the brilliant idea of leaving the gate of this pasture open, so that the strange cattle that ran at large might drift in to feed on the grass there. When they had lured the cattle into the pasture they would close the gate and ride and rope to their heart's content.

This was an exciting game and they might have gone on with it indefinitely, but one day at round-up time, "Doc" Frazier missed some of his cattle. After looking all over the country for them, he found them at last in the pasture being ridden and roped by a crowd of shouting boys.

"Doc" Frazier was furious at first and threatened to take the boys' ropes from them. Will, realizing how serious this would be, decided to try to save the day by diplomacy. "Aw, Doc," he said with a disarming grin, "we didn't mean any harm. Anyhow you ought to be proud of them cows now. We've got 'em all gentled and broke to ride!"

The boys kept their ropes but they had to abandon the school pasture as a roping place.

In the winter this pasture was sometimes flooded by rain which would freeze over, leaving the whole plain smooth and level. Then there would be moonlight skating parties. Some of the boys had horses that were shod and would not fall down on the ice, and they would hitch these horses to a sled and give the girls the ride of their lives, or, with the girls holding on to long poles, the boys would pull them around over the frozen pasture. At all these festivities Will Rogers was one of the leading spirits and could always be depended upon to think up new and daring things to do.

About this time Will had trouble with another boy— one of the rare times when he became really angry. Marshall Stevens, one of his schoolmates, lost a favorite necktie and seeing Will in the Annex wearing one of the same color, he went up to him and demanded that he give it up. Will indignantly refused and at once the two boys began to scuffle. The other boys parted them but Will was so angry at having been accused of theft that he packed his clothes and left the Annex, going to live at the home of Mrs. Miller at the edge of town. Later, Marshall Stevens found his missing tie and apologized to Will. The two again became friends but Will did not go back to the Annex.

At this new rooming place he shared a room with Mrs. Miller's son, Roy, and soon came to feel quite at home. He was becoming more and more particular about his clothes and now purchased his first pair of long trousers. He insisted that Roy Miller should wear long trousers too, and though at first Mrs. Miller objected, she finally yielded to the coaxing of the two boys.

The long trousers marked an epoch in Will's life—he was grown up. He now took dancing, art and elocution in addition to his regular studies and took considerable pride in them. He once won a medal in a reading contest. There were seven pupils in the contest and no one thought Will had any chance. But Miss Crooms, the elocution teacher, knew what he could do if he tried, and coached him thoroughly.

In spite of the fact that he was no longer a little boy, he still had a little boy's love of pranks, and played them constantly on everyone around him. His wit was developing too, though of course it did not have the keenness and maturity that it did in his later years, but it amused his friends and school mates and very often came to Will's aid when he might otherwise have found himself in trouble.

Underneath all his fun and love of pleasure lay the pride and sensitiveness that sometimes caused him to be deeply hurt. On one occasion Mrs. Miller gave a birthday party for one of her children and sent out invitations to all the child's friends. On the day of the party Will Rogers dressed himself in his best clothes, but when the boys and girls gathered at the house, Will was missing. A search was made for him and he was found at last, running along the tops of a long string of empty box cards, down on the railroad track. The children coaxed him to come to the party but he refused. Three times Mrs. Miller sent for him and each time Will made some excuse and stayed where he was.

When the party was over he came in as usual. "Why did you act that way, Will?" Mrs. Miller asked him.

"Why didn't you come and play with the children?"

"Because you didn't send me no invitation," he told her.

"Why, Will," Mrs. Miller laughed, "I didn't think it was necessary to send you an invitation. You're one of the family."

But Will shook his head slowly. "I couldn't come," he said quietly but definitely. "You didn't send me no invitation."

And now his three years at Willie Halsell college were drawing to a close. During this time his father had seldom interfered with him, but had allowed him to work things out for himself. Will had his own ideas about things and his father was wise enough to let him make his own decisions whenever possible. Thus the boy had been thrown on his own resources at an early age and it was this, perhaps, that gave him the strength of character which he possessed to such a marked degree in his later life.

Measured in terms of scholastic achievement, his three years at Willie Halsell school had perhaps been wasted years. But Will Rogers had grown in other ways. He had not made much headway with his studies, but he had made many friends. He could not easily adjust himself to the routine of school life, but he had learned to make a life for himself—a road of his own along which he must walk.

Chapter 9
SCARRITT COLLEGE

IN THE summer of 1895, Professor J. C. Shelton traveled over the Indian Territory by horse and buggy, looking for new students for Scarritt College of Neosho, Missouri. He called at the Rogers home among others, and there he made such a good impression as he told of the advantages of Scarritt, that Clem Rogers decided this was just the school for Will.

"Papa, I'm tired of going to Willie Halsell," Will had told his father earlier in the summer, hoping to be permanently divorced from all schools.

"All right son," Clem had replied and Will's heart bounded with hope. But it quickly sank again as Clem continued, "If you're tired of Willie Halsell we'll have to find you another school."

The visit of Professor Shelton had solved the problem for Clem, and once more Will had to resign himself to another year of school.

Neosho, a rocky little town surrounded by forests of black oak, with walnut and hickory in the valley, lay in the edge of the Ozark mountains just over the line in Missouri, seventy-five miles from the Rogers home. It

was a Methodist Episcopal Church South school and
its president, Doctor Charles Carroll Woods, was an
ex-Confederate soldier with a splendid reputation as a
school man.

When Will Rogers made his first appearance at this
school he was a long-legged gangly country boy whose
two-year-old clothes fitted him like a scarecrow. The
cuffs of his trousers struck him just below his knees,
the bottom of his coat usually crawled up around his
waist, his coat sleeves ended just below his elbows and
the funny little hat he wore looked like the relic of
another generation. But in spite of his strange-looking
garments, he was so good-natured and kindly that he
soon became a favorite with his school mates.

There were three other Indian Territory boys of
Cherokee blood in Scarritt that year—Dennis Keyes,
Gordon Lindsay and Billy Walker. Will knew these
boys well and the four of them at once became fast
friends.

The discipline at this new school was much sterner
than at any of the other schools Will Rogers had
attended, and it was rigorously enforced by the
president, Doctor Woods, a tall, thin and very dignified
man who walked with a stoop and wore a frock coat
that reached to his knees. He was a kindly, learned
man and his chapel talks contained much homely
wisdom, but his strict enforcement of the rules of the

---

school and his rather straight-laced ideas, soon irked the four Indian Territory boys.

Shortly after school opened a circus came to Neosho, and that morning in chapel Doctor Woods took occasion to issue a warning to the students. "I want no absence from school today on account of the circus," he said. "Circuses do not amount to anything. All you will see there is a beautiful young lady wearing an extremely short skirt and riding on the back of a dappled gray horse, one foot resting on the horse's back and the other pointing to the North Star."

This was enough to decide Will and his three Indian friends, and they promptly cut school for the day and went to the circus. They were each given ten demerits for this breach if discipline, which did not bother them in the least. The circus had been worth it.

Will was as poor a student at Scarritt as at any of the other schools to which he had gone. He did not study at all and, consequently he seldom knew a lesson or passed an examination. He made no secret of the fact that his ambition was to become the best cowboy in Oklahoma, and that he had not come here because he wanted to but because his father had sent him.

He refused to be serious about anything except riding and roping, but these he worked at increasingly. He spent a great deal of time standing in Wood Street, having the country boys ride their horses past him so that he could rope them, while crowds of students and townspeople looked on. Although his arm was still stiff and crooked from his accident of the summer before, his roping was as good as ever and his rope seldom missed its mark.

Although he was a poor student and impatient of any restraint, his teachers liked him and usually were lenient with him. But there came a week when he cut classes so regularly that the faculty decided to make an investigation. Professor Shelton, who understood boys pretty well, thought he knew where he would find Will. He had heard some cattle bawling in the loading pens down at the Kansas City Southern Railroad, and had an idea that this was where Will would be. So he set off to find him.

Sure enough, there was Will, having the time of his life. He had borrowed a little gray mare from Bill Johnson, a stock buyer, and as fast as a steer would escape from the yards, Will would ride after it and round it up. If the steer became too rambunctious Will would take the fight out of it by dabbing his rope on it and throwing it. All the men at the stock yards were sitting around admiring the skill of this school boy who knew so much about handling a rope and who could yell at a steer just like an Indian Territory cowhand.

HIS AMBITION WAS TO BECOME THE BEST COWBOY IN OKLAHOMA
(Courtesy Will Rogers Memorial and Birthplace)

When Will saw Professor Shelton, he did not say a word but, climbing off his horse, he quietly accompanied the professor back to the campus, his holiday over.

The college had a military unit called the Scarritt Guards. Its members wore neat uniforms of Confederate gray and drilled regularly with old discarded Springfield rifles which the Government had loaned them. The Reverend Will G. Beasley was chief officer and Will Rogers was a private. He was awkward, wore his uniform badly and cut drills every time he found a chance, but when called on the carpet by his superior officer he was so blandly innocent that, although often the officer was exasperated, he could never deal very harshly with the boy.

During the first few months at Scarritt Will had almost no close friends except the three Cherokee Indian boys. But as time went on and he began to feel more at home, he bought some new clothes and presently began to go about a little with the girls, as he had done at Willie Halsell. He taught them songs in Cherokee and made them laugh by his pranks and funny stories, so they liked him even though he was different from the other boys they knew. They nicknamed him "Wild Indian."

The students at Scarritt were forbidden to attend the performances of the traveling stock companies that came, now and then, to Neosho, but Will Rogers seldom missed any of them. He would borrow a suit of old clothes from Wiley Sims, pad himself with a pillow, blacken his face and hands and put on false hair, and thus disguised, he would steal down town and into the Negro gallery of the old Neosho Opera House. Later, he would come home, and, to the astonishment of his roommates who were not familiar with his amazing feats of memory, he would repeat the show almost word for word.

In spite of breaking so many rules and playing so many pranks, Will managed to avoid getting into serious trouble with the faculty except once, and that time he came very near being expelled. The escapade grew out of his habit of roping anything and everything that crossed his path. He roped his schoolmates, he roped fence posts, dogs and cows. Anything at all over which his singing rope could drop was considered fair game to Will. But once he went too far.

One Saturday morning he put on his big hat and, with his rope in his hand, he sauntered out looking for fun. Dennis Keyes and Gordon Lindsay soon joined him and Will, spying Professor Shelton's bay colt grazing in a nearby tennis court, dropped his rope on him.

The colt immediately became frantic with terror. It reared and plunged and pawed the rope with its front

THE COLT REARED, PLUNGED AND RAN THROUGH THE
BACKSTOP OF THE TENNIS COURT

legs. It laid down and rolled over and over, all the while neighing shrilly. The three badly scared boys swung desperately onto the end of the rope while the colt, now on its feet once more, knocked over a picket fence and ran through the backstop of the tennis court. Finally they managed to get the rope off of him and then they ran for all they were worth.

In the meantime, Professor Shelton, hearing the neighing of the colt, came to investigate and, for a moment, he thought the colt had been killed. Doctor Woods, the president of the school, sent at once for the three boys and gave them the severest lecture any of them had ever had.

"I have had much experience in educational circles," he concluded, "but I have never before in my life seen anything like this. You boys are incorrigible rule-breakers, and must be punished."

He was on the point of expelling them when Will Rogers, who had done the roping and therefore felt that he must do the talking, began to plead with Doctor Woods, promising solemnly not to do such a thing again.

The president listened to him and at last promised to wait a while before doing anything definite. "I will take it under advisement," he said, and with that the boys had to be content. He was wise enough however, to keep them in suspense until the end of the school term, and during that time the three boys behaved so well that no one could find any fault with them.

The following autumn Will returned to Scarritt, but he had not been there long when his brother-in-law, the husband of his sister May, was assassinated back in the Indian Territory. Will went home to the funeral and did not again return to school.

His stay at Scarritt had been as unprofitable as his stay at other schools, and many of his schoolmates soon forgot this boy who gave so little promise for the future. He was neither a student nor an athlete; he was not a musician nor an orator, and they never dreamed that he would someday be the world's most famous humorist, a beloved motion picture and radio star and a great humanist, who would steady thousands of drifting people.

Years later the Reverend Beasley wrote of him: "There were brilliant students in that school who gave promise of success and achievement, and have since fulfilled that promise. But even the most sanguine could not have predicted that the funny fellow we knew as Will Rogers, would be anything but mediocre, or live anything but an absurdly uneventful life."

Chapter 10
A SUMMER AT HOME

WILL ROGERS was growing and developing rapidly. He was giving more and more thought to his personal appearance and now began to have his boots made by Old Man Woodson at Claremore, the best boot maker in the country, and whether he was on horseback or afoot, Will Rogers always wore spurs. He did not like the wide "six gallon" hats so much affected by cattle men of that day, but preferred a narrow-brimmed hat with the top crushed in. His boots and his hats were his especial pride and he always took great care of them.

As his body developed, so did his mind and personality. He was always a fearless boy and so absolutely unafraid of anything that he was regarded as slightly reckless by those who knew him best. He was learning to think and reason well, and often talked himself out of the difficulties he got in because of his love of playing pranks.

The older black boys, Ike, Bud and Anderson Rogers and Mack Walker, had built a springboard overhanging a pit of water in Mose Walker's coal mine, and because Will was such a daring boy and so full of fun, these boys often invited him to go swimming with them. The water in the pit was blue and clear and was about fifteen feet deep in the middle, and Will would often do flip-flops off the springboard, talking always in his droll way so that he kept his companions laughing constantly.

One morning as these boys were enjoying a swim, their swimming hole was invaded by Charley Craynor, a white boy, and his gang who peeled off their clothes, jumped in the water and began to swim. All went well until Will and his friends started to leave the water, but as fast as they would get out of the pool Charley and his gang would throw mud on them so they would have to go back into the water to wash it off.

At first Will and his colored friends took this good-naturedly, but by and by they grew tired of it and began to throw mud too. This mud-throwing contest developed rapidly into a fight and Charley Craynor and Anderson Rogers engaged in a hand-to-hand combat, beating each other with sticks and fists and growing so angry that a general row threatened.

Then Will Rogers stopped throwing mud and began to make peace. This was difficult because the Negro boys were now as eager to fight as were their opponents, and Will had to placate both factions.

He began to talk to them but Charley Craynor cut

him short.

"Yah!" he jeered, "what's the matter with you? Are you gittin' scared? Well, let me tell you we're gonna fix you and them niggers with you!"

Will was not frightened by this threat. He did not lose his head but kept on arguing in the serious, compelling way he had and, after a bit, he somehow succeeded in making everyone listen to him in spite of themselves.

"Now boys," he told Charley and his gang, "you can't whip me and you know it. I could whip the whole bunch of you put together but I hope that ain't gonna be necessary. What good's it gonna do you to fight us anyhow? And besides, look what we're fightin' about— a few hands full of mud!"

Charley and his friends began to look sheepish. They stood there digging their bare toes into the mud and said nothing, but Will kept on talking and grinning that infectious grin of his and presently Charley Craynor was grinning a little too, though he probably could not have explained why. It may have been a reluctant admiration for Will's gift of gab. Boys everywhere are quick to recognize and respect any kind of talent in each other, and one of Will Rogers's best talents was talking.

"All right," Charley said at last, "we'll listen to you." Then Will turned to his friends who stood just behind him with fists doubled and angry looks, hot and eager for battle.

"Now boys," he said to them, "I want you to listen too."

He was as successful with his own friends as he had been with Charley and his gang, and soon he and the colored boys got out of the pool and into their clothes, and the incident was closed. He had simply talked both sides out of their desire to fight.

This summer at home passed quickly for there were always plenty of things to do. Sometimes Charley McClellan would get up a "stomp dance" and Will would help him. They would hold the dance on a slight elevation on the prairie, near Oowala just north of Charley's home, and they would work for days snaking logs on horseback to the scene of the fun, and picking apples from the Rogers orchard with which to make cider to be served, ice-cold, from a tepee on the ground.

Will and Charley and the other boys would put bands of red cloth around their heads and paint themselves up like Indians, and presently the girls became so interested in these dances that they made themselves Indian dresses out of cambric, and painted themselves as the boys did. Naturally, Charley McClellan loved this kind of play and Will, who loved it almost equally well, was always at his elbow, helping him every minute.

Although in many ways Will was growing more mature, he did not give up his teasing and liked nothing better than playing jokes on his friends and acquaintances. One night he and "Doc" Payne went to Oowala to a pie supper. At these suppers the boys would buy the pies which the girls had baked, and each boy ate supper with the girl whose pie he bought. One of Will's friends was George Collins, the druggist at Oologah, who was then going with a girl named Pink Drake. Naturally George wanted to buy Pink's pie so that he could eat supper with her. Will Rogers knew this and deliberately set about preventing it. Not only did he outbid George for Pink's pie, but he and "Doc" also impishly prevented George from buying a pie from any of the girls.

When the bidding was over, Will and "Doc" had eight or ten pies while poor George had neither pie nor girl. He was justly angry, of course and told the two boys what he thought of them. But Will only grinned at him and said: "George, if you buy anything tonight you're gonna have to soak your drug store to do it!"

Another of his pranks ended more disastrously. On a windy day, when he and "Doc" Payne were riding horseback to Oologah, Will pulled two cigars out of his pocket. "Let's smoke," he proposed, and though "Doc" was surprised, for Will never smoked, he accepted. Both boys were inexperienced in smoking and had to strike a half dozen matches before they succeeded in getting their cigars lighted.

When they had ridden about fifty yards farther on, "Doc" chanced to look back and his face froze with fright. "Gosh!" he yelled, "what a fire!"

It was true. Behind them the yellow flames were crawling and crackling out over the dry prairie, fanned by a steady wind. The two boys thought of the hundreds of acres of wild prairie hay that lay in the path of that blaze. For a few minutes they fought it themselves, but it was too much for them so they soon gave up and rode their ponies at a dead run back to the ranch.

There they got Mose Walker and a man Charley Deskin, and while Mose and Charley and "Doc" loaded gunny sacks and barrels of water into a wagon, Will rode out to the pasture to find a horse to pull the wagon. The only one he could find was an old blue horse that never had been broken to a wagon. But Will herded him in anyhow, hitched him up, and soon they were off across the prairie, Will lashing the horse with the ends of the lines. The horse, doubtless a little surprised at what was happening to him, obeyed his driver nevertheless, and broke into a gallop.

All day long they fought that fire, backfiring and using other means at their command to stop its progress, but in vain. Will Rogers worked harder than anyone. For once he did not talk—he only worked and sweated and panted. Everyone in the little party fought desperately, for more than one farmer's supply of winter feed was imperiled by that blaze.

The old blue horse that had been pressed into action was not at all excited. He behaved perfectly. When the going was the hottest he sat down in the harness and spread his front feet out, laid his ears back and stared curiously at the blazing prairie like some gawky country boy. He appeared to be having the time of his life.

The flames burned up a great deal of hay—most of it Clem Rogers's—before the fire was finally extinguished at about nine o'clock that night. At last, exhausted they threw themselves down in the wagon and rested.

Clem Rogers was away from home on business at this time, which everyone considered lucky for Will. As they lay panting in the wagon, Mose Walker wiped his face with his bandana, looked over at Will and grinned.

"Well, Will," he said, "if we hadn't got that fire out I reckon we'd have had to set up with you tonight."

"Then you'd have had to set up ridin'," Will replied instantly, "because I'd shore been gone!"

After that day Will was never again interested in smoking.

Will had inherited his mother's tenderness and

compassion, and there was nothing he would not do for the sick or unfortunate. One day word came to him that Anderson Rogers, the colored lad that he had played with from a boy, had lost an eye and an arm in a shooting accident near Catoosa.

Will Rogers did not hesitate a moment. He saddled Comanche and galloped to Rab's creek where Anderson's father had brought him home. Tears ran down his cheeks and anguish showed plainly in his face when he saw the pitiful figure Anderson presented.

"You come on home with me, Anderson, where I can take care of you," he proposed through his tears. But the colored boy only lay there, a sullen look on his face. He was ashamed of his stump and his empty socket and thought of going through life with only one arm and one eye. Never again would he fork a bronc or squint down a rifle barrel. No one would want to have anything to do with an ugly one-armed fellow. Why, his own folks would be ashamed of him.

Will, realizing what Anderson was thinking, offered to buy him a mechanical pop-corn machine and set him up in a pop-corn stand in Claremore. But Anderson, sensitive, dazed and still brooding, answered bitterly that he "didn't want to be no monkey and sell peanuts."

Will was not offended at this refusal of his offer. All he could think of was the terrible misfortune that had befallen his friend. He tried to cheer Anderson up, joked with him and told him he would soon be around, although tears were running down his own face as he spoke.

"After you get up and your stub gets well, I'll buy you an artificial hand," he offered, and taking some bills out of his pocket he laid them on the bed. Then he went out and talked to Anderson's father, telling him that if Anderson would go to some high-class colored school and learn a trade, he would pay for it.

"I couldn't have had a brother that treated me any nicer than Will Rogers did," Anderson said afterward. "He rode over to Catoosa and told George McKeehan at the drug store and Tom Daugherty at the grocery to let me have anything I wanted and send the bill to him. And they did."

Thus we get a pretty clear picture of Will Rogers at about the age of fifteen. While he was noisy and mischievous, he was an affectionate, fearless, good hearted boy who was now learning to express himself well and who was staunchly loyal to his friends.

Chapter 11

KEMPER

C LEM ROGERS had not given up his determina-
tion to have Will acquire an education. He still
believed that Will could get some good out of schooling
if only a school could be found that would hold his
interest.

After a good deal of thought Clem decided on Kemper
Military Academy at Boonville, Missouri. The school
had a fine reputation and in those days many well-to-
do ranchmen sent their sons there, not only for the
academic training the school offered, but also that
they might acquire poise, learn obedience, manliness
and how to be orderly in personal appearance. There
were the sons of many prominent families at Kemper
when Will Rogers went there, among them Burton
Mudge, son of the president of the Santa Fe railroad;
Alden Nickerson, whose father was president of the
Mexican and Central railway; Norris Beebee, son of a
well-known Boston leather manufacturer; R. D. Wil-
liams, son of a judge of the Missouri Supreme court,
and many others.

Will arrived at Kemper on January 13, 1897, wearing

107

full cowboy regalia, a short Stetson hat with a braided horsehair cord, a flannel shirt, red bandana hand-kerchief around his neck, a richly colored vest and high-heeled red-top boots with noisy spurs. Several coiled ropes were strapped to his luggage. He must have looked strange to the Kemper boys, clad in their trim uniforms.

One of the first boys Will saw was John Payne, also part Cherokee, whom he had met and known at Tahlequah when their fathers went there to the Cherokee Council, years before.

"Why hello, John," Will drawled, beaming because he had found someone from home, "they got you here, too?"

"Yes," laughed John, "I'm servin' time same as you."

Since both were new students and John had no roommate, he and Will shared John's room on the third floor of the rambling three-story brick building that housed the academy. The Kemper school was located on the edge of Boonville, an agricultural town of ap-proximately four thousand people. The school itself was situated in a pretty spot, with hills and native timber all about and the Missouri river just half a mile away.

Although Will was still a very erratic student, he did better than he had at the other schools he had attended. He was near the head of his class in history in his last four months of school though his grades once fluctuated from 100 down to 68 in one month. He was also good in letter writing, elocution and political economy; in fact he always did best in talking subjects where he could argue with his teachers. Despite his uneven pace, his monthly average ranked close to the school average which was a decided improvement for him. But he still disliked study and would often snatch up a book on his way to the recitation room, examine the lesson and, because he had such a good memory, he would make a fine recitation.

Will probably got more fun out of the elocution class than any other. The teacher was Professor Annin, a sandy-haired little man from Princeton who wore a Van Dyke beard. In those days every expression called for certain gestures and Professor Annin was very particular that the students should get the right ones and also the correct voice modulation. This was Will's chance to have some fun and he always was pretending to get the wrong gesture. He looked so ludicrous saying one thing and gesturing another that it was impossible to keep order in the classroom when he was on the floor.

Will took a great interest in the school activities and in the fall he went out for football, making the second team at end. But his fondness for pranks had such a demoralizing effect on the other players that he was usually kept on the sidelines. When his eleven went into a huddle, Will was apt to break forth in some of the gestures he had learned in his elocution class, and the players who had studied under Professor Annin would, of course, recognize them and time would have to be taken out for a laugh. At other times when some team mate would be crouched in the line just before the snapback, Will would reach over and push him on his face. So Will's football career was never very notable and he spent most of his time watching the games from the bench.

The Kemper authorities outfitted each cadet in beautiful gray-blue uniforms with braid down each side of the trouser legs and around the collars and sleeves. The caps were blue with heavy patent leather peaks and gold braid initials KS on the front. They had smart looking dress uniforms with "spike-tailed" coats and round brass buttons. They wore these uniforms to church and it was one of Will's favorite tricks, when a boy started to sit down in the pew in front of him, to kick his studded coat tails under him and then look innocently at the preacher as the uncomfortable cadet rose to readjust his coat tails and scanned the seats behind him for a guilty face.

Will wore his uniform carelessly, in spite of its splendor, and was always reporting for inspection with his coat unbuttoned. Another of his frequent

THE KEMPER BLUE GRAY CADET UNIFORM

crimes was being out of his room after taps. When the nine-thirty bugle blew, he would probably be in some other boy's room pouring water in the bed or playing some other prank.

But the officers could never be very angry with him. Even when Colonel Johnson, the commandant, wanted to reprimand Will and would shout, "Mr. Rogers, stand up!" Will would rise and look so sorry and repentant, and would say, "Yes, sir," with so much contrition that the Colonel would have to turn his head and laugh.

He loved his joke and would go to almost any extreme to have it. Once, when his platoon was drilling near the school lake and the inexperienced young corporal who was giving the commands turned the platoon too close to the water and was so flustered that he did not give the command to halt, Will, who was on the end of the line, threw down his gun and keeping perfect step, walked into the water. As it rose above his stomach he gave a loud whoop and swam out, amid roars of laughter.

"Will's uniformly good nature occasionally gave way to anger," wrote Lieutenant Colonel A. M. Hitch, the author of the excellent pamphlet, "Cadet Days of Will Rogers." "He had Indian blood from both his father and mother—and was very proud of it. Once a classmate referred to a certain Indian chief as a thoroughbred. Will's voice rose to a high pitch of resentment as he explained that 'fullblood' was the proper term, and that it spoiled his whole afternoon to hear someone call a fine Indian a "thoroughbred."

At one time there was a strike at Kemper. Some of the cadets felt that the officers were pulling the strings a little too tight and urged their schoolmates to strike. About two-thirds of them finally walked out, Will Rogers and John Payne among the number. In speaking of it later, John Payne said: "Will and I figured we might as well join them because, after the first month of school, we had got into so much mischief that they had taken away all our privileges, anyhow. We all went down town and stayed until our money gave out and we had to start rustling for ourselves. Will said 'The Boss (Clem Rogers) won't send me any, but I can get some money from my sister Sallie.' But before he could ask for it, we got so hungry that we finally appointed a committee to treat with the school heads and we went back. There wasn't any compromise. They skinned us good!"

During his days at Kemper Will kept up his roping practice, and his skill was the talk of the academy. He was always playing with his rope and would beg his fellow cadets to "run and beller like a calf." When they did this Will would rope them expertly and if, after a while, they grew tired of it he might even pay them a quarter to rouse them to further effort. He still played pranks with his rope and once, when he saw a uniform coming around a corner he quickly swung his rope, only to discover that he had lassoed one of the officers. This mistake cost him many demerits.

Will had acquired a surprising skill at Oropeza's stunt of spinning vertical and horizontal loops and stepping in and out of them to suddenly flip the loop over a running boy's foot or arm or neck. Even in the classroom where he had to keep one eye on the teacher and the other on the target, he was deadly with a quarter-inch cord which he carried in his pocket. If a boy two seats down would stealthily stick out his hand and indicate which finger he wished roped, Will's tiny loop would always settle over the designated digit. He could even catch his classmates by their ears.

Because he got into so much mischief, Will was frequently compelled to walk guard, the most common punishment for demerits. Later in his life in speaking of this, he said: "I was two years at Kemper, one in the fourth grade, and the other in the guard house." And at another time he told Harry Osborn, one of his old friends at Scarritt, that he had so many demerits at Kemper that when he left he owed the academy one hundred hours of marching time.

The spring season was always hard for Will, as it was for Ben Johnson, John Payne, Bill Johnson or any of the Kemper boys who had been raised on a ranch.

When the blue grass began to spring up on the campus, and the new leaves budded and the birds came back, Will and Ben Johnson would stand out in the sunshine with their arms around each other, talking of home and of how soon work would start on the range. There the colts and calves would be coming through the branding season, and the ponies would be shedding and growing sleek and fat, and everyone would be getting ready for the round-up.

It was a call that both longed to answer; a call that Will Rogers would soon answer, for he was restless and wanted to wander around like a pony with its bridle off. He was tired of Kemper; tired of struggling with its rigid military routine with little change or variety, ten months in the year. The newness had worn off and he was ready to push on.

He had talked a great deal to Bill Johnson, a boy who came from a ranch near Canadian, Texas, in the panhandle. Bill was a good scholar and a crack mathematician, but he was also a real Westerner who had been raised in the cattle country.

"Why don't you go out to Perry Ewing's ranch at Higgins, Texas?" Bill asked Will Rogers one day. "You'll like it out there. The Ewings are fine folks and they'll let you stay. They've got a boy named Frank who's a good one. He don't like school any better than you do. Why don't you go out there?"

Will thought it over and decided to go. He wrote a letter to his sister Sallie asking for a loan of ten dollars, and one to his sister Maud, asking for the same amount, and each sister promptly sent him the money he asked for. It was enough to pay his fare to Higgins, Texas!

And so one night Will Rogers ran away from Kemper. He was through with schools forever. For years he had been irked by their routine to which he could not adapt himself, and now he was determined to lead the free life he loved so well.

Back at Kemper the janitor brought Will's trunk down to his room and John Payne silently packed Will's things so that they could be shipped home, while the other cadets stood watching him sorrowfully. They had all like Will Rogers and were sorry to see him go.

Chapter 12
A PANHANDLE COWBOY

W HEN WILL ROGERS climbed off the Santa Fe train at Higgins on a clear sunny day in February, 1898, the clean, pungent smell of sage from the Texas prairie was wafted to his nostrils. He took long, satisfying whiffs of it and grinned. It was good to be out in the open again.

He stood in the nippy air and looked about him with interest. Higgins was a raw young panhandle town that looked as though it had been built in a day and set down on the dusty prairie. It had a handful of stores and about two dozen dwellings, each with a wooden windmill in its back yard to harness the boisterous wind and make it pump water for household purposes.

Will's eyes traveled with interest down one side of the street and up the other. He saw a saloon, Old Man Prickett's boot shop, Gray's law office and Winsett's big mercantile store. Across the street from them was the Peugh store and the old two-story Higgins hotel. And that was all there was to the town of Higgins save for the depot and a little corral south of the railroad, where the town liveryman pastured his horses.

On all sides the tan prairie, a vast expanse of wild grass, seemed to flow and fade into the distance. Will Rogers's eyes lit up curiously when he saw that prairie, for it was different from any he had ever seen before. It seemed wilder, flatter, more endless and

FRANK EWING

undisturbed than his own prairie back on the Verdi-gris. Its grass was short and matty, and it had the sweetest air he had ever breathed.

Inquiry revealed that the Ewing ranch was twelve miles south of Higgins, on Little Robe creek, and that the Ewings only came to town every two or three weeks for provisions and mail. However, Will was told that the Winsetts, who lived in Higgins, were relatives of the Ewings, so he hunted them up and stayed with them until he could get out to the Ewing ranch.

It was not long before Perry Ewing heard that there was a boy at Higgins who wanted to get to his ranch, so he drove into town and took Will home with him. A twelve-mile buggy ride across the prairie was a long trip in those days, but Will Rogers enjoyed every foot of it. The south wind rippled the dead buffalo grass and quail whistled from the sage. Once they passed a little bunch of cattle that raised their heads to stare at them, and Will got a tremendous thrill out of that. He seemed starved for a sight of ranch life and was craning his neck during the entire ride.

It was not long before he got his first sight of the Little Robe, as the Ewings called their ranch. It was named for the creek that flowed through it, and the creek in turn was named for a noted Cheyenne chief who had ranged in that area and later fought in the battle of the Washita. The ranch itself consisted of thirteen thousand acres of rich buffalo, meadow and river grass; as fine and fertile a ranch as could be found in the whole country. For nine miles on the southwest it was bound by the South Canadian river, whose glassy surface Will could see glinting in the sunshine several miles away. As they rode along Perry Ewing pointed out everything to the excited boy.

When at last they reached the house, Frank Ewing, Perry's young son, was waiting for them. "None of us had ever seen Will Rogers before," Frank said years later, "but that didn't make any difference to him. He jumped right out of the buggy with a grin and helped me unhitch the team. He was a big boy and wore a red-and-black striped sweater; maybe it was a football sweater. It was late in the afternoon but we stayed out in the barn for a while and talked. Will told me all about himself, who he was, and where he'd been, and that Billy Johnson of Canadian had sent him to us. 'I was about to be expelled from Kemper,' he said, 'and I figured this was once I'd just beat 'em to it.' He was smiling all the time and seemed glad to be there. I liked him the first minute I saw him."

Will pitched right in and worked like one of the hands; in fact he could see work that the other hands never looked for. He wrangled the horses up in the morning, helped with the round-up and helped the neighbors with their branding. He was never lonely but always smiling and happy as a lark.

He soon found that Frank Ewing was all that Billy Johnson said he was, and more. Frank was a husky, friendly youth in whose quiet blue eyes lurked a hint of deviltry and fun. Like Will Rogers, Frank hated school. The only one near him was a combination cabin-dugout, taught by Frank's eighteen-year-old brother Rees, which Frank haughtily refused to attend. Not only did he refuse to attend, but he spent much time hanging around the outside of the school house just to torment the pupils.

Once he smoked them out by putting a board over the chimney, and another time he emptied the school room even faster by riding past and roping the ridge pole that supported the structure. The pupils saw him from the window and, fearing a total collapse of the rude building, emerged like a swarm of bees.

But Frank's father, who was a fiery Kentuckian who could rule his family, now took a hand and sent Frank back to school. Reluctantly the boy went—but not for long. Sooner there came a Friday afternoon program and Rees Ewing announced that each pupil must give some kind of reading. When it came Frank's turn he protested that he had not had enough warning, but Rees was insistent. He could not have the pupils going home and telling their parents that the teacher granted favors to his brother.

So, with a glint of mischief in his eyes, Frank got up and recited as follows:

"Oh Lord above, look down with love
    On us poor sinful scholars.
    Who hired a fool to teach this school
    And paid him thirty dollars."

That ended Frank's schooling permanently. No one asked him to come back.

Being in many ways so much alike, Will and Frank soon became inseparable. They would get up before daybreak and go out to drive the horses up so the cowhands could select their mounts for the day. They would have tugs of war on their ponies, with a rope stretched tight between their saddle horns and each pony pulling his best. They worked cattle together and occasionally "busted a steer" when Perry Ewing wasn't looking.

Sometimes they would go to Higgins for supplies, or ride to Grand to attend a country dance, though neither of them danced. But they would sit around, listening to the squeak of the fiddles and the clanking stride of the square dancers. They would talk to the girls and gorge themselves on the food and coffee that was always served at midnight. And when the dance broke up they would ride all night under the stars and get home just in time for breakfast.

After a time Perry Ewing wrote to Will's father, telling him where Will was and how he was getting along. "I would advise you to leave the boy alone," he wrote. "He's doing fine here. If it is agreeable to you, he can stay here and I'll keep him at work." In a few days a letter came, postmarked Oologah, Oklahoma. "He likes to roam," Clem wrote Perry Ewing, "but keep him there as long as he'll stay and work. If he needs money, draw on me."

When Will had been at Little Robe a month, Perry Ewing paid him his first wages—the thirty dollars that every top hand drew in those days. Will Rogers looked surprised.

"What's this for?" he asked.

"Your wages for one month," Mr. Ewing told him.

"Aw, I wasn't workin'," Will protested, "I was jest visitin'."

It was never easy for Will to keep out of scrapes but now, with Frank Ewing to aid and abet him in any kind of deviltry, it was inevitable that they should get into trouble. One day the two of them were riding along the river and came to a little bunch of cattle under a tree.

"Let's see which one can tie down first," proposed Will. No sooner were the words out of his mouth than each touched spurs to his horse and the contest was on. Frank picked out a big, fine-looking steer, rode past him and jerked him off his feet. But when he ran up to tie him, the steer lay there was a broken neck. Sobered and considerably scared, Will and Frank mounted their ponies and rode for cover as fast as they could, for Frank's father had just ridden by a few minutes before and he might return soon.

That noon Perry Ewing said at dinner, "A strange thing happened today. I was riding past a bunch of stock over by the river this morning and saw a fine fat two-year-old standing under a tree. Thirty minutes later I rode back the same way and he was lying dead not far from where I had seen him. I can't figure it out."

Will and Frank, feeling very uncomfortable, looked down at their plates and pretended to be engrossed with their dinner. Nothing more was said and the boys never confessed what they had done but it had been an anxious moment for them.

And now began a new phase in Will Rogers's development. He began to read anything and everything he could lay his hands on. Perry Ewing was a great reader and always kept up on politics. He took the "Wichita Eagle," and the "Kansas City Star," and Will always read both of them entirely through. He also read the "Police Gazette" which he bought at the post office in Higgins or read in the barber shop.

He was so happy and contented with the Ewing family that he kept on "visiting." He liked the climate, the panhandle people who were friendly and hospitable, and he liked the country. It was the kind of life he had dreamed of in those days at Kemper, and he had no regrets at all that he had left his school days behind him forever.

Chapter 13
TRAILING A HERD TO KANSAS

T HE SPRING soon came. New buffalo grass sprang up green and thick on the prairie, covering the little canyons and gulleys so beautifully that soon the whole land looked dimpled. The days grew warmer, and out on the range the new-born calves were frolicking in the sunshine. Prairie chickens crowed from the sage.

Perry Ewing had four hundred head of cattle, a mixed herd of cows and calves and yearlings that he wanted driven to Medicine Lodge, Kansas, about a hundred and sixty miles northeast. There he had leased a pasture and planned to fatten the cattle on Kansas grass for the Kansas City market. He decided to put Frank, who was then only nineteen, in complete charge of the herd, while he himself stayed behind to complete arrangements for the shipping.

Frank quickly assembled the outfit, which included a chuck wagon, a remuda and seven hands. Besides Frank and Will Rogers the outfit contained Will Poleman, a German; Dude Porter, a young cowhand from Higgins; Aaron, the cook, and a couple of boys to wrangle horses. Aaron was a quarrelsome, dangerous fellow who had once killed two men in knife fights, but in spite of his bad reputation Frank Ewing decided to take him along because he was such a good cook. The herd gathered at Mr. Ewing's northwest camp on Camp creek, north of Higgins and, early one May morning, the start was made.

The cattle made a pretty sight as they serpentined up and down the long rolls of land that seemed to rise in crests and sink in hollows. Although they were allowed to scatter at will, they were always grazed forward and never permitted to take a backward step. In the morning they would be thrown off the bedding ground and grazed a mile or two, then bunched and driven a mile or two before a stop would be made for dinner. Then they were rested and watered and at three o'clock gathered and driven until sundown. It was a routine from which they would actually gain weight if grass and water were plentiful.

It was exhilarating to a roaming young fellow like Will Rogers to ride up a long, green, sage-dotted slope with the thought that over the top would be new unseen country. Since the remuda consisted of thirty-five head, each cowhand had six or seven horses to ride. Will would have loved to have Comanche along, but he had a good string of horses that included Anchor, a little red roan Spanish pony; Panther, a big sorrel, a good horse, but mean; Rooster, Button, and K.T., a little one-eyed brown horse that Will grew very fond of.

At night the outfit would take turns riding guard, with each hand taking a three-hour shift. Will Rogers had the nine to midnight turn and then it was his job to wake Dude Porter and go back to the herd until Dude came to relieve him. Then, and only then, could he turn in.

But Dude was the sleepiest trail-hand that Will had ever seen. He would wake up, talk to Will and then, after Will had gone back to the herd, he would turn over and go to sleep again.

Presently Will got tired of this, and one day he complained to Frank Ewing. "Dude Porter's the hardest guy to wake up I ever saw," he said, "I've been standin' from a half to three-fourths of his guard on top of mine and I'm getting' darned tired of it."

"Hm," considered Frank. "I'll tell you what you do," he said at last. "Next time he does it why don't you drag him out?"

It was a suggestion that appealed strongly to Will and he put it into execution the very next night.

It was a beautiful moon-drenched night and deathly quiet—almost depressingly so. No coyote's wail nor owl's screech disturbed the night's perfect peace. All around, the thick curly buffalo grass lay glistening in dewy splendor and Will could hear the cows, full of grass and water, and lying down, grunting and breathing and belching softly. Even the cricket's song had died to a tranquil drone and, as Will rode slowly around the herd, it was not hard for him to imagine that he was the only person alive in some strange world.

Soon his watch showed that it was time to rouse Dude Porter for the next guard. Will strode over to where Dude lay on the prairie with a tarpaulin pulled up under his chin. Dude had pulled off his boots, his California pants and his Stetson hat, and was sleeping in his shirt, socks and his "long handled" Scrivenger drawers that every cowboy wore, no matter how hot the weather.

Will leaned down and shook him by the shoulder.

"Hey! Wake up, Dude! Time to go on guard!"

Dude stirred and stretched. "Aw rite," he muttered thickly.

"Are you awake?"

"Yeah."

"Sure you're awake?"

"Yeah."

Will rode back to the herd and waited. But Dude didn't get up. Will waited a little longer and still no Dude. Then he quietly rode his pony to the foot of Dude's bed and swung off, his saddle rope in his hand.

Raising the tarpaulin, he fixed his noose firmly around Dude's ankles, mounted and spurred his horse. He was riding Anchor, the spirited little roan.

Frank Ewing had been tipped off in advance and was watching from his bed roll. He saw them leave, one end of the taut rope fastened to Will's saddle horn and the other to the threshing body of Dude Porter who was being snaked along through the wet buffalo grass like a load of wood. Will dragged the shouting Dude one hundred yards before he ever pulled Anchor to a stop.

Dude, now thoroughly awake, was so angry that he wanted to fight, but Will looked him right in the eyes and talked straight to him. "Now Dude," he said, "I've been havin' to wake you three and four times every night since we started. I ain't gonna do it any more. Every time you don't get up I'm gonna pull you out of there just like I did tonight."

Behind them they could hear Frank Ewing laughing so hard that he was rolling in his blanket and, without another word, Dude went back and changed his thoroughly soaked clothes and resumed guard. For the rest of the trip no one ever heard him called twice.

The drive went on. The cattle were trailing splendidly, making five or six miles a day. As trail boss, it was Frank's responsibility to select the route, and they never got lost. They trailed sixty miles to Fort Supply before seeing a fence, and there they cut straight

THEY ALWAYS TRIED TO CAMP BY A CREEK OR A SPRING

through the Cherokee outlet.

Each morning after breakfast the herd would go on and the horse-wrangler would help Aaron, the cook, load the bedding and hitch up. Soon the cook would catch up with the rest and Frank Ewing would tell him where to stop for dinner and when they came up at noon, dinner would be ready.

They always tried to camp by a creek or a spring at noon, so they could have water. But this was not always possible for sweet water creeks were few and far between. The water problem proved a difficult one and often the water barrel on the side of the chuck wagon was empty and they would have to open a can of tomatoes and eat them to quench their thirst.

"I'll never forget how Will could eat," Frank Ewing remembers. "He never got enough. Aaron was a good cook and when we tumbled out at daybreak for breakfast, he'd have black coffee, sow belly, molasses and sour dough biscuits baked in a Dutch oven all hot and ready for us. Sometimes we'd buy loose boxes of dried blackberries. They'd be wormy, but we'd sort out the worst and cook the rest.

"Once in a while we'd pass a little ranch and buy butter, milk and eggs and have us a feast. There was lots of wild plums in those days, and we'd gather 'em in our hats while horseback, or just eat 'em off the bushes. Once in a while the cook might gather 'em in a dishpan

ROUNDING UP THE CATTLE IN A SUDDEN PRAIRIE STORM

and make us a cobbler in the Dutch oven."

One night just before sundown Perry Ewing, on his way to Medicine Lodge, overtook them in his buggy and stayed all night. "You're doing fine, son," he told Frank after checking the outfit carefully. And the next morning he rode on.

Just before they reached Salt Fork, one of the sudden prairie storms for which this country was noted, struck them in full fury. Each man put on his slicker and had no difficulty in keeping dry, but the general concern was for the cattle which were apt to be stampeded by thunder, lightning and hail. If these cattle could be held together until they got good and wet, they would not be so likely to run, so at once the men bunched them and stood guard over them.

The rain beat down so hard it nearly pounded the brims off their hats; the brilliant prairie lightning flashed and was followed by thunder detonations so loud that they seemed to be fired from some giant cannon. Some of the hands were so frightened that they unbuckled their spurs, threw their pocket knives on the ground and then moved away from them. But presently the storm passed without doing any damage to them, and the dreaded stampede of the cattle did not occur.

But now the muddy water ran, bank full, down each draw and creek, and the prairie was over-run with prairie dogs that had been driven from their holes by the water. The men tried to force the cattle to cross Salt Creek, which was up and roaring, but the cattle would not cross, so it was decided to lay over for a day.

The second day they tried again and this time were successful, though it was not an easy task for man or beast. "Finally we threw part of the remuda in ahead of 'em and they went a scattin'," Frank Ewing later said. Like everyone else, Will Rogers got soaking wet during the crossing. He was riding point and it was his job to keep the herd strung out and headed right so they would not cut back or mill. The cattle made a pretty sight when, at last, they were all in the river, swimming with only heads and horns showing above the surface of the muddy water.

Trail life, with its long hard days and its arduous nights, placed a heavy strain upon the men who followed it, and before many days everybody was so on edge that to provoke a man at all meant a fight. And now, with tempers strained to the breaking point, Aaron, the cook, who had killed two men in his day, began to grow surly.

He had plenty of reason for this, for some one of the men on night guard had been turning the alarm clock ahead to escape his three hours night guard duty. The trick was not discovered for a while and consequently the last night guard, who was supposed to waken

Aaron at four o'clock each morning was, instead, summoning the cook at two o'clock.

When at last it was discovered that the clock was being turned ahead, Aaron was furious and brooded over it until he was ready to explode. He did not know who it was that had played the trick on him and eyed everyone with a suspicious eye. This was not pleasant, for in addition to his bad reputation, he always wore a dirk in a scabbard in his hip pocket.

One night when Will and Frank Ewing were bedding down a little bunch of cattle and Will went to the chuck wagon for a drink, Aaron hotly accused him of being the one to turn the clock ahead. Will denied it, but Aaron paid no attention and began cursing and inviting a fight.

Will Rogers did not back up a step. Sitting astride his horse he looked steadily at the infuriated cook. "They tell me you're a killer," he said tauntingly, his voice vibrant with scorn, "but you're not. You're just a plain murderer. You haven't got nerve enough to fight. If you have, come on out here," and he motioned to the prairie behind him.

Will was a pretty husky youngster at that time, five feet and eleven inches tall, and weighing a hundred and seventy pounds, and he was angry. So Aaron, after looking him over for a moment decided he had made a mistake. There was no fight.

At the end of six weeks they had reached Perry Ewing's pasture, ten miles east of Medicine Lodge, without having lost a single animal. It was a fine showing and, by way of celebration, they rushed to town for a haircut and a civilized supper of ham and eggs. The return was eventless and they covered it in about five days.

When they got back to the Northwest camp near Higgins, Will Rogers again became restless. He was always looking for new country. He stayed another week with Frank Ewing, but all the time he was uneasy, and at last he told Frank that he believed he would push on toward Amarillo and try to get a job there.

Frank hated to see him go but, knowing Will, he knew it would do no good to protest. He gave Will a horse, Old Gray Eagle, big-kneed and crippled, because Will would not take a good horse, and the two boys said goodbye.

Once more Will Rogers was on his way.

Chapter 14
DAYS AT OOLOGAH

WILL ROGERS rode the eighty miles from Ewing's Northwest camp to Amarillo in three days, and climbing off the old gray horse he looked around him. Amarillo, named for the profusion of yellow flowers that covered the panhandle prairie in the springtime, was a rough cattle town of about twelve hundred people, and its main thoroughfare, Polk Street, was a road lined with board sidewalks and hitching racks. With the coming of the Fort Worth and Denver railroad, in 1887, this little town had become the largest shipping point in America.

Will learned that a large herd, owned by Light Knight and Henry Slayton of Plainview, was being held just outside the town, bound for Liberal, Kansas, and the the northwest. He decided to try to get a job as a hand and finding Pres Burnam, trail boss of the outfit, he asked: "How'd you like to hire a new cowboy?"

Burnam explained to him that the oufit was filled, but that if he would go to the Amarillo hotel and look up Light Knight, one of the owners, he might get a job. Will did this and Knight, liking him at first sight, hired him.

He and Burnam, the young trail boss, immediately became good friends and were together a great deal during the drive through the northern half of the panhandle. Will chewed gum and talked incessantly, while Burnam, who was a quiet retiring young fellow, only listened. One night Burnam sang a song called "The Cowboy's Dream" whose first line was, "Last night as I lay on the prairie and looked at the stars in the sky." Will liked this song instantly and did not rest until he had learned it. It was the first "dogie" song he had ever heard and it became a great favorite with him.

When they reached Liberal, Kansas, Will quit the outfit. It had not taken him long to learn that trailing a big herd was not very different from trailing a small one and, since he had already had that experience, he was restless and anxious to move on.

For the next two or three years Will never seemed to know quite what he wanted to do. He sold his horse and saddle and "rode the blinds"—the front end of the baggage coach—to New Mexico, and then to Trinidad and Pueblo, Colorado. There he encountered cold weather and heartless train crews. One night, when he attempted to ride on the front end of a baggage car, the train crew put him off only to have him run and jump back on again. This happened so many times that it finally became a contest between him and the crew. He managed to get back on the train each time and when it became dark he found a way to ride undisturbed. There was a chicken coop lashed to the front end of the baggage car. With the train going thirty-five miles an hour, Will opened the end of the coop, tossed the chickens out and crawled inside the coop to ride, unmolested, until daybreak. He never forgot the startled cackling of those hens as they sailed out over the countryside to freedom.

In September of '98, he turned up again at Perry Ewing's Northwest camp and stayed there until December, and then decided to go back to Oologah for Christmas. It was the first time he had been home in a year, and Clem was glad to see him and give him a new start.

Clem, then fifty-nine years old, was busy with his new duties as a member of the Dawes Commission. Honors had come to him thick and fast. In June, 1893, he had been appointed by President Grover Cleveland, as one of a commission of three to appraise the improvements of white settlers in the Cherokee nation. He had served four terms as senator from the Cooweescoowee district, beside his single term as judge. His political duties took much of his time and he was glad to have Will at home to help with the ranch.

When the Curtis Act became mandatory, abolishing all free range in the Cherokee nation, Clem Rogers organized a bank at Claremore, moved there and after re-stocking the farm, left it in charge of Will. He himself had owned his own herd and had run a trading post as well, at the age of seventeen, and he did not see why Will, who was now nineteen, could not handle the ranch.

Will stayed around home for several months, passing the time in a variety of ways. For a while he worked

CLEM ROGERS, TO WHOSE LATTER YEARS
HONORS HAD COME, THICK AND FAST
(Courtesy Will Rogers Memorial and Birthplace)

hard and Clem thought he had perhaps turned over a new leaf. But presently Will's restlessness overtook him and he began to prowl around at night, saddling Comanche and riding over to attend the dog and pony shows that sometimes came to Oologah, or running around the neighboring country with his old chum, Charley McClellan.

Soon Clem and Will began to have arguments because Will did not pay closer attention to the ranch. Clem had never had the love of roving that was so much a part of Will's nature and he could not understand it. But he had learned that Will was hard to argue with and that he intended to go his own way and live his own life.

One day Will went to Claremore and told his father that he wanted to give up the responsibility of the ranch, and Clem could do nothing but let him go.

A few days later Will left for Higgins, Texas, traveling by his new method—"riding the blinds." When he reached his destination and climbed down from the front end of the baggage car, the white suit he was wearing was black with coal smoke from the engine. It was election day and Frank Ewing happened to be at the depot when Will arrived. "Why, hello there, Will," he said. "What are you doing here?"

"I came back to vote," grinned Will as he brushed the dust from his clothes.

Will went back to the Northwest camp with Frank and, as they rode along, he told of his dispute with his father. He seemed to be glad to get back to the panhandle country and stayed for several weeks with Frank, in the one-room sod house on Frank's claim, and helped with the work around the ranch. But after a time he again grew restless and wandered back home once more. It was a time of indecision for him. He did not seem to know where he wanted to go.

Often Clem was out of patience with him. "Will," he would say sternly, "you can go back to the ranch and take care of the cattle or you can starve."

"All right, Papa," Will would answer good-naturedly, and he would go back to the ranch and try to become interested in his work. But all the time he was squirming inwardly. He wanted, more and more, to go his own road and do as he pleased.

Once, during this period of unrest, Will got into difficulty and was placed under arrest, because of his unwillingness to submit to discipline. Oologah was under quarantine for smallpox, and in those days a smallpox scare was enough to throw any town into a panic. Buck Sunday, a friend of Will's was mayor of the town, and he and the town council decided to make the quarantine strict. People were forbidden to get on or off trains, and all roads leading to Oologah were blocked with quarantine signs.

But this did not stop Will Rogers. He wanted to get his mail and so, saddling Comanche and taking Gordon Lane, a friend, with him, he boldly galloped into town. George Speaks, the town marshal, ran out into Main Street to stop the two boys but Will, paying no attention to him, almost ran him down.

Wrathful and excited, Speaks rushed over to Buck Sunday and reported. Buck, only twenty-three and a good friend of Will's, was in a dilemma. But there was only one thing to do—he ordered Speaks to arrest Will the next time he came to town.

A day or two later the marshal came striding excitedly into Buck Sunday's store. "Well, I've got Will Rogers," he told Buck exultantly. "Got him down at Beck's store. I want you to come down with me."

There was nothing for Buck to do except accompany his deputy. Will, with Gordon Lane beside him, was standing in front of a hitching rack, holding Comanche's reins. His face lit up when he saw Buck. "Well, Judge," he grinned amiably, "what are you goin' to do with me?"

"Will, what's the matter?" Buck asked, sparring for time.

"Well," answered Will, still grinning, "I tried to run over your marshal, but I couldn't catch him."

Buck Sunday was terribly embarrassed. He dropped his eyes and drew aimless lines in the dust with the toe of his boot. "Will, we've got a quarantine. Did you know that?" he said at last.

"Shore," admitted Will, "but I wanted to get my mail."

Buck shook his head as though the excuse was not good enough.

"Will," he said sorrowfully, "I'm gonna have to fine you."

Will Rogers laughed. He saw Buck was suffering and felt sorry for him. "Aw, that's all right, Buck," he told the young mayor. "How much?"

"It'll be the regular rate for two," said Buck. "Nineteen dollars and sixty cents.:"

"Will you take my check?" Will asked.

"Yes, I'll take your check, Will," Buck told him.

Borrowing the marshal's pen and using Comanche's saddle for a desk, Will wrote the check. "Here you are," he said, handing it to Buck, "and if I get the smallpox, I'll ride over and give it to you and the marshal!"

Will held no grudge over this incident and, years later, he asked Buck Sunday to be his business representative in Oklahoma, and Buck served him wisely and well.

When he was in Oologah, Will Rogers spent a great deal of time at the Missouri Pacific depot. In those days there was something alluring about a depot in a small town and, like several other young fellows, Will liked to loaf there. He liked to see the station agent swing the ruby semaphor when a whistle screamed inquiringly down the track, and he liked to see the passenger train come roaring through the night, the coach lamps dimmed and sleepy people sprawled across the plush seats. He liked to hear the busy clatter of the telegraph key, and the pleasant whine of the wire.

Bill Marshall was then the agent at Oologah, and he and his wife lived in the back of the depot.

One day a new girl came to Bill Marshall's depot home to visit. She was Betty Blake of Arkansas, a sister of the agent's wife. Moreover, she was pretty and quiet and attractive.

Soon after her arrival it got so that Bill Marshall could hardly turn around in the depot without stepping on some boy who had heard about the new girl who was visiting here and had sauntered casually over to the depot in the hope of getting a look at her.

Will Rogers was one of these boys, but nobody paid much attention to him. To the average citizen of Oologah, Will was a likable fellow who had been a great many places but who would probably never amount to very much. He was a boy who liked to ride broncs and rope pigs and chickens and people, just for a prank. He was apt to come into town with one trouser leg slit, a heel missing from his boot and his saddle rope dragging on the ground. He was so plain and ordinary and full of his own fun, that nobody could take him seriously.

But Will saw the girl as she sat in a rocking chair on

the back platform, and liked her. So he immediately set about trying to impress her. He displayed his fancy roping for her benefit and, one day, he even drove an old white-faced steer into town, roped it, threw it down, hog-tied it and then waved his hat, all right in front of the depot. But Betty Blake gave no indication she had seen him. She only sat there and rocked.

Nearly thirty years later Will Rogers told of this incident in Oologah. Speaking from a wagon box in Main Street, he made a confession.

"Why," he said, "do you know I ran that old steer out on the prairie for three hours, before I could get him tired and slowed down enough to bring him to town and throw him in front of Betty!"

But his efforts were not in vain and, evidently, Betty Blake was not so oblivious of him as she pretended to be. For, some years later, she married this steer-throwing young cowboy, who tried so hard that day to impress her.

Chapter 15
JIM RIDER AND THE "JOHNNY BLOCKER"

IN THE year 1898, steer ropings, or what are now called rodeos, came into popularity and Will Rogers began to find an outlet for his energy and his roping skill.

The steer ropings were impromptu gatherings held out on the prairie, with the crowd sitting around in wagons and buggys or on horseback to watch the fun. No one attended on foot. If anyone had attended an early Indian Territory roping on foot, he might have had to climb a tree in order to see—and trees were scarce!

Steer roping and bronch riding were the chief sports at these gatherings. Bulldogging and calf roping were unknown, but roping a steer and riding a bucking horse were things every Indian Territory cowhand had to learn first if he worked cattle. So it came about naturally that these cowboys began to vie with each other at roping and riding, on Sundays or holidays, and out of this sprang the ropings and little Wild West shows that eventually became the modern rodeos.

Steer roping is hard and dangerous work and requires the utmost skill of both man and horse. When cowboys wished to throw a steer out on the range, one man would rope him by the head and another by the heels, and they would string him out and tail him down. But contest roping was faster and different. The steer was turned loose and headed for open country and, when he crossed the chalked line, the watches started and so did the ropers.

If the roper's horse knew its business it would go, like a bullet, to the left of the steer and stay there until the cowboy roped the steer by the head. Then the horse would dash on past the steer and, as he passed, the cowboy would turn to the left and yank the steer off its feet, stunning it. As soon as he felt the shock, the horse would back up and keep the rope tight, and the roper would leap out of the saddle, snatching a short tie rope from his belt as he ran, and securely tie together three feet of the fallen steer. When he had finished this, the cowboy would throw up his hands and the judges would snap their watches. The roper who could do it in the shortest time, won the prize money.

Will Rogers began going to the ropings held nearby. He attended one at Vinita in 1898 but won no prize. He also went to the St. Louis Fair the same year, shipping Comanche, but the little dun cow horse was green at contest roping, and let the steer knock him off his feet three or four times. However, it was good experience for both Will and Comanche.

"I don't hope to win anything," Will said later, "I jest want to get acquainted and get started."

Will won his first steer roping at Claremore on July 4, 1899. The "Claremore Progress" described the event as follows:

"Last on the program, and most exciting of the day's sports was the roping contest. Ten entered but only a few of them were in any way successful. Will Rogers won first money, roping and tying his cow in 52 seconds. Sam Dickenson won second in one minute 19 seconds. The other candidates had bad luck of one kind or another and failed to get in the race."

To Will Rogers this meant more than merely winning. It started him out on a perfect spree of ropings. After that, whenever he heard of one he would go to it no matter how far away it was. He loved to rope and he loved to travel and, unlike most of the other Indian Territory boys, he had plenty of time and money to do both.

He never stinted himself on equipment. He usually had the best saddle, boots, blanket and spurs that money could buy, and if he saw a horse that he wanted, he would try to make a deal for him on the spot. He soon became a fine judge of horses, and a shrewd horsetrader, too.

Once, when he was at Tahlequah at a roping, he saw

Hick Miller tie a steer in thirty-four seconds, on a big bald-faced sorrel horse, with a white mane and tail. Will saw immediately that here was real horse—quiet, smart, and stocky enough to throw any steer that ever lived, and to hold him after he threw him, too.

"Is that horse for sale?" Will asked Miller after the roping.

"Oh," shrugged Miller, "I don't care about sellin' him, but I will."

They did not agree on a price that day, but Will was persistent. He started out at $75.00, went to $100.00, and finally to $125.00. And at the mention of this price Hick Miller took the saddle and bridle off the horse. The name of the horse was Robin, and it was one of the best horses Will Rogers ever owned.

Will now spent his entire time practicing roping. He and Spy Trent and Dick Paris built a log house on the top of a hill, a mile west of the Rogers home, and lived there. They wanted to be alone so they could practice steer roping. In the heat of the day they would sit about strumming a guitar and singing, but when it got cool they would go out and rope the big steers in the Rogers herd. Although Will was still nominally the boss of the ranch, his sister May and her husband Frank Stine, lived in the old home and looked out for things. Someone had to look out for them, for Will was usually off attending steer ropings.

Between ropings he would sometimes ride over to the Jim Hall ranch to see Jim Rider, a young cow-puncher who worked there who was related to Hall. Once Will arrived there just in time to see Jim Rider start branding eighteen hundred yearlings that Hall had shipped from Texas. He did not stand around watching, or ride back home. This was work he dearly loved so he stayed a week, helping rope and brand the

JIM RIDER, A COWPUNCHER PAL OF WILL'S

whole herd. "Naw, he wasn't working for wages," Jim Rider recalled later. "Will would probably have paid Hall to let him go in there an' rope those calves."

Will now attended ropings everywhere. Sometimes he would enter them as a contestant and other times he would do trick roping in front of the grand-stand. Occasionally he did both. He and Spy and Dick Paris, Ernest Schrimsher and Charley McClellan attended a big roping in Oklahoma City, July 4, 1900. None of them won any prize money, but they did see Theodore Roosevelt, then just back from Cuba, and were introduced to him before the roping.

Will Rogers helped greatly in the development of Jim Rider as a contest roper. Jim was just a boy like Will, but in his raw, homely face was the mature look of a man twice his age, and he spoke the salty language of the range. He knew cows and he knew roping. He was the only boy roper anywhere around who was a skilled user of the "Johnny Blocker," a crack Texas throw, in which the loop was turned over instead of being sent out flat. Where a flat loop will sometimes bounce off a steer, the "Blocker" snaps up fast, closing all the time. It is also a good head throw, especially effective on "muleys"—cattle without horns—or shorthorned cattle. Jim had learned it from Link Purcell, foreman of the Hall ranch.

Will always felt sorry for Jim Rider because Jim

never got to go around to the steer ropings. He was working for wages and was too busy roping steers on the range to fool around with professional roping. But as he occasionally lounged around the stock yards and watched others load their horses and boisterously climb aboard the train to go to some roping contest, there was a wistful look in his eyes that hurt Will Rogers to see. He thought a lot of Jim and worried about him. Jim wasn't having enough fun.

Will had seen Jim throw the "Blocker" in the branding pens and felt sure that he was as good as eighty percent of the contest ropers. Eager to see Jim in action at the contests, Will wrote him inviting him to the Pryor roping on July Fourth. "Don't worry about horses," he said, "I'll have Comanche and Robin here and you can use them."

Jim Rider decided to go. At Pryor Will Rogers, Jim Hopkins and Spy Trent met him. "Will, I've never seen a steer hawg-tied in my life," Rider protested, with his homely grin. "I ain't never been to no ropin's, so I don't even know how to tie a brute down."

"Shucks, Jim," snorted Will, "that's nothin'! I've got all that figured out. Now listen. All the ropers draw numbers out of a hat to see who ropes first. If you come ahead of us, we'll trade numbers with you so you'll be the last one of our gang to rope. When we tie down, you come out and turn 'em loose for us. That way you'll learn how to make your wraps."

Jim did just as Will Rogers told him to, and as he untied for his friends during the first day's competition, Will gave him hints on how to tie.

When they called Jim's number Will Rogers held his breath, because the best roper on the range is not always best in a contest. But Jim Rider went after his steer as coolly as though nobody was there but him and the horse and the steer. Using the deadly "Blocker," he nailed his brute, threw him and tied him. He was a little clumsy on the tie, but he did it in fairly good time at that. And he got in the money! He did not win but he placed.

Will had been bragging about how sure Jim was with a rope and when Jim did not win first money, Will was in for a good bit of kidding. "I thought you said he could rope," the cowboys taunted Will. "Why, he just scratched. He just threw his rope into the air and the cow run into it."

Will Roger's pride in his friend ran hot. Although he seldom bet, he ran his hand in his pocket and pulled out a great roll of bills.

"Yeah?" he retorted. "Well, I'll have him scratch again tomorrow. And I'll bet any part of this that the cow runs into his rope again!"

This sobered Jim's critics and they did not take Will's bet. The next day they were still more sobered when Jim Rider won second money in a field of crack ropers. Again he used the deadly "Blocker" but this time nobody made fun of it. Instead, they marveled at it and, after the roping was over, they tried to get him to teach them. Soon Jim was the busiest boy in Pryor.

When Will Rogers and Jim got back home, Will led him off behind the barn where they would not be interrupted.

"Say, Jim," Will began, "will you do me a favor?"

"Shore," answered Jim Rider. "What?"

Will shot a look over his shoulder to assure himself that nobody was looking, and bashfully kicked at a corral post with his boot.

"I want you to show me how to throw that Johnny Blocker," he grinned.

Chapter 16
LATER ROPINGS

AT THE Confederate reunion in Memphis in May 1901, Will Rogers tried his hand at promoting, and was one of four who underwrote the cowboy roping. The event was well attended but so poorly managed that Will and his partners lost considerable money on it.

Colonel Zack Mulhall, who was one of the underwriters, brought along his daughter Lucille, a slim girl of fourteen, who could rope and tie a steer as fast as any man. Will Rogers met this girl who was soon to become the outstanding cowgirl of all time.

As usual, Will and his friends had a great time in Memphis. They went up in a day coach, sleeping in the seats and using their saddles and saddle blankets for pillows. For amusement they roped all the men passengers who came through their car on their way to the dining car. "Sorry, but you're not allowed to go through there now," they would say, expertly roping their victims, who took their prank good-naturedly.

Will did not do any roping at Memphis, but acted as "barker" for the roping contests and announced them from the grandstand. He was also given charge of arranging the program and straightway he got into trouble. Since the roping was to last six days, beginning on Monday, it was Will's idea to offer a big free show the previous Sunday to introduce the ropers to the spectators. This was not a bad idea. But in order to impress the big crowd doubly, Will decided to select ten of the best ropers, himself, to insure a fast contest. Right there his trouble began.

He selected among others, Heber Skinner, Gordon Lane, Hurt Flippin, Dick Paris, Jim Hopkins and Jim Rider. The selection of these men naturally miffed the men left out. But they were fully revenged later on, for it was their job to select the steers to be roped and they chose the biggest and wildest ones they could find.

The ropers had never seen such mean steers. Dick Paris broke his rope when he went on one side of a tree and his steer on the other. Hurt Flippin's steer crashed through the fence and ran clear out of the fair grounds, with Hurt hot on its trail, and when they found them a few minutes later, a quarter of a mile from the scene, Hurt had thrown and hog-tied his steer on a lawn in the residential district and was sitting on him, mopping his brown with his bandana.

But Jim Hopkins's steer put on the best show of all. Will Rogers, speaking from the grandstand, had given Jim a real introduction. It was so flowery that even

WILL SPINS A LASSO AROUND HIMSELF

Jim, who was by nature a sulky fellow and usually went around looking like a thunder cloud, permitted himself an extra hitch of his belt and a more exaggerated tilt of his big white Stetson hat, and rode like the wind when they turned his steer out of the chute.

But now Jim had a bit of hard luck. He roped his animal all right, but when he "busted" him the saddle girth parted, spilling Jim to the ground. The loose saddle flew up in the air and, rebounding like a broken sling shot, hit the fallen steer squarely in the face. This was an affront that the half-stunned animal could not overlook. While the crowd roared with mingled mirth and alarm, the steer leaped to its feet and made a run for Jim Hopkins. Jim had to think quickly and, seizing the saddle he squatted under it, scarcely daring to breathe. The steer was puzzled by this ruse. It stopped and smelled at the saddle for a moment or two and then disgustedly turned and trotted away, dragging Jim's saddle with it. And now the laughter swelled from the grandstand like thunder.

It was an afternoon of weird roping, but much hilarity and fun. Jim Rider, who had speeded up his tying, won first money that day. Turning his steer in front of the grandstand, Jim put the "Blocker" on him. With thousands of wide-eyed spectators looking on only a few yards away, Jim threw the steer and tied him in forty-five seconds.

Will Rogers was so excited that he was jumping up and down. "That's good! That's good! Put 'em up!" he yelled at Jim, but Jim Rider always tied them tight. When he finally did put up his hands his steer was bawling, but Jim had him wrapped up fine.

Will jumped over the fence and caught Jim's horse by the bridle rein. "Come on," he commanded, "I want to introduce you to the crowd." Jim hung back, but Will pulled him to the inside track in front of the grandstand. "Ladeez and gentlemen!" he shouted. "This is Jim Rider from Talala, the ropin'est scoundrel in the Territory!" But just as Jim lifted his hat to the crowd as Will had instructed him to, some urchin up in the grandstand piped shrilly, "Keep cool, Jimmy!"—and Jim Rider's rout was complete.

Jim Hopkins was still so peeved over the mishap of the broken saddle-girth that for days he would not speak to anyone. But this mood was only the brooding melancholy of a great roper who was girding himself for a supreme effort. Before the Memphis show had ended, he borrowed Will Rogers's pony, Comanche, and rode out to rope and tie a steer in eighteen seconds flat, breaking the world's record.

It was an astonishing performance by both man and horse, especially as a roper in those days did not compete on race-horse stock, gave the steer a sixty-foot start instead of the twenty allowed now, and had to take down his rope, build a loop, catch his steer and take at least three wraps and a half-hitch on the tie before he could raise his hands.

WILL ROGERS TIES DOWN A DOGIE STEER

Again Will Rogers was more elated than if he had made the record himself. He was proud of Jim Hopkins, just as he had been proud of Jim Rider. He was proud of little Comanche, too.

At the Elk's convention at Springfield, Missouri, in September of that same year, Will Rogers entered the roping contest and gave the finest performance of his life up to that time. He tied in fifty seconds, being beaten only by Jim Hopkins who tied in forty-five. But the second day Will defeated Hopkins with a mark of forty-four and was beaten only by Bill Orms of Tulsa, who roped and tied in forty seconds flat.

The cowboys probably pulled more crazy stunts during this Springfield contest than they had at any of the others. During the street parade they roped girls by the feet, they roped conductors off of street cars and even roped the street cars themselves. And if anyone took offence at such treatment, they would joke them back into good humor.

Charley McClellan was the star of the parade. He rode at its head wearing a beaded vest, leggings and mocassins and a full head-dress of eagle feathers that dragged in the dust of the street. He had even brought along old Bubba, his favorite pony, and had plaited eagle feathers in the pony's mane and tail, painted his hoofs red, and had daubed a red streak along the line of his mane.

The cowboys, wearing purple shirts, were the center of attraction. The town was turned over to them and everyone was very hospitable to them. One day, after a roping, they were so tired that they tumbled off their horses in the shade on a big blue-grass lawn, and turned their horses loose on it to graze. They expected hostility from the owner, but instead of this the men came out and visited with them and the women brought them lemonade and cake.

The cowboys found plenty of new things to see in Springfield, and they usually did their sight-seeing at night. According to the "Springfield Republican," the sights of the Midway at the Elk's carnival were many and wonderful. They comprised, among others, glass blowers, the biggest man on earth, weighing seven hundred and fifty pounds, Esau devouring rattlesnakes, the streets of Cairo with an Egyptian theater featuring Saida Mohamed—"princess, priestess and dancer," an electric fountain costing ten thousand dollars, and "Lunette, the Flying Lady." The cowboys saw them all.

In spite of the fact that Will Rogers was in the midst of all kinds of temptation, with vice running rife around him, he kept his head. "He was as clean a boy as every lived," Heber Skinner once said of him. "He was clean in every way. He was as clean as you could ask a boy to be."

Will's last steer roping in 1901 was at the San

Antonio International Exposition, during October. He and Jim Hopkins made the trip together and contested against some of the wickedest steers and finest ropers in all Texas. Will finished eleventh in a field of nineteen in the second day's roping, tying in one minute and thirty-six second. He drew a black steer and wasted three loops on him before he finally threw and tied him.

While in San Antonio Will met Clay McGonagill, a big, jovial Irish cowboy, of whom he was destined to see much in his later show life. McGonagill, so old-timers say, was the luckiest cowhand in Texas. At Juarez, in 1900, he is said to have won both the roping contest and the bucking horse contest and, while other ropers were standing around eyeing him jealously, Clay McGonagill raffled off his horse and saddle and won them too!

Charley Tompkins, another roper and showman of whom Will was to see a great deal in later life, was also at San Antonio at this time, and later gave a vivid account of something that happened to Will.

"The climax of the exposition was a three-steer roping contest," he said. "Will was on the Indian Territory team. On his second trial he roped his steer all right, but his saddle turned on him. The steer jumped over the center field fence into the race track, and it took Will seven minutes to land him. It was fatal to his

team, and after he'd tied the steer his pride was hurt
so badly that he leaned against his horse and cried,
right there on the race track in plain sight of everybody.
He couldn't keep the tears back. The other boys patted
him on the back and told him to forget it, that his team
probably wouldn't have won anyway. But Will was
humiliated and disappointed."

Back at Claremore Clem Rogers was worrying a
good bit about Will. He did not like him to be running
about the country so much, and besides, Will had been
spending money pretty freely and that worried his
father too. Clem was not close about money but he
hated to see it thrown around carelessly. When Will
returned home, Clem talked to him about this, and
though they had something of a quarrel, they soon
made it up and were friends again.

Possession of a herd and the management of his
father's ranch had not cured Will Rogers of his vagrant
tendencies, and soon after this he made up his mind to
leave home and go to South America.

One day he rode over to tell Jim Rider of his plans.
"I had a fine 'Walker' saddle," Jim recalls, "made out of
California oak-tanned leather with raised flowers hand
stamped all over it. Will took a fancy to that saddle and
wanted to buy it. He spent three days trying to talk me
out of it. We'd ride around on our horses, Will talkin'
and me listenin'. He argued that I could get another

saddle, and finally he wore me out and I traded. He gave me his saddle, several Navajo blankets and fifty dollars in money."

Will Rogers left Comanche with John Lipe, sold his little herd of "dogies" and invited Dick Paris, the Tahlequah roper, to go with him to South America. "I'll pay your way out there," he offered.

"Yeah," grinned Dick Paris, "but I might want to come back."

"Well," replied Will, "I'll tell you what I'll do. I'll pay your way out there and back."

It was a deal. Will Rogers would be gone almost three years on this trip. In his fidgety feet was a powerful itch that nothing but transoceanic travel would satisfy.

Although he did not know it then, he was leaving the beautiful Indian Territory forever. Never again would he live in the land of his birth.

Chapter 17
ARGENTINE

WILL ROGERS and Dick Paris did not have an easy time getting out of the United States. They went first to New Orleans where they were told there was no boat bound for South America. Then they went to New York but learned there that the Buenos Aires boat had gone. They were advised that the quickest way would be to go to England and from there to Argentina, so they sailed on February 1, 1902.

Although he seldom wrote letters when he grew older, Will was a prolific letter-writer as a young man of twenty-two, and the most authentic record we have of his trip is contained in the letters he wrote to his father and to his sisters Sally and Maud. These letters were later reprinted in the "Chelsea Reporter," the small weekly newspaper of the town in which Sally and Maud lived.

His first letter back home, dated from Southampton, England, April 4, 1902, reveals his budding humor and penchant for striking observations of foreign manners and customs. He says that his baggage was searched for tobacco and spirits, but they didn't find any as he

168

didn't chew, and his spirits had all left him on that boat. He was taken by a hansom, not a lady but a kind of cart, to a hotel where he got a nice room almost papered with pictures of Queen Victoria, who "must have had a stand-in with the photographer." He complains about the food which was different both by name and by nature; he almost starved for something cooked in America. Evidently his stomach was still thinking about that boat.

Seventeen years later, in an article printed in the "American Magazine," Will Rogers again described his seasickness on that first voyage, and the contrast in his humor at the age of twenty-two and forty is interesting.

"Well, I broke all records for seasickness. I just lasted on deck long enough to envy the Statue of Liberty for being in a permanent position and not having to rise and fall with the tide. When we stopped off Sandy Hook to let off the pilot, I never wanted to trade jobs with a man so bad in my life. . . . I landed in England with the sole purpose of becoming a naturalized citizen until some enterprising party built a bridge back home."

Will and Dick were ten months getting from England to Buenos Aires. They arrived there May 5, 1902 and stopped at the Phoenix, an expensive English-speaking hotel. But after Will had paid eight dollars a day for a week, and had taken time to count his remaining money, he gave up the idea of buying a ranch.

He did, however, want to find out how the Argentinians handled cattle, so he and Dick left for the interior by rail, with a view to seeing the large Argentine ranches and getting a job, if possible.

In a later letter home he said that it was a beautiful country—"the prettiest I ever saw"—but no place to start in unless one had ten thousand dollars to invest. He couldn't find any other American cowboys, so he felt lonesome.

Soon the two young men began to be disillusioned, for the country was not all they had expected. Dick was the first to weaken, and on May 23, Will wrote that Dick was to start back to America soon, and that he himself had been for a trip into the interior and didn't like it. "I am liable to show up any minute," he says, "so look out."

The letter does not reveal that Will Rogers had used up almost all his money buying Dick Paris's passage home, in accordance with his original promise. Before long Will himself began to feel pangs of homesickness similar to Dick's, although in a letter dated Buenos Aires, June 9, he could still jest about the situation. However, a careful reading of this letter leads one to suspect it is pretty serious jesting. He says that the country was overrun with cheap labor; the first year you are supposed to work for nothing. And as for working with cattle, the American boys couldn't compete with natives, for the Americans couldn't speak Spanish, couldn't live on their food, or make out on five to eight dollars a month in American money. He himself had given up the idea of making any money there, but he "wouldn't take a fortune for his trip." His best advice to the boys back home was, "just stay where you are; marry and settle down!"

That his contempt for the Argentine method of working cattle was very great is shown by a letter from Buenos Aires in July, 1902, in which he says that they didn't use any judgment in handling a bunch of cattle. They would run them so hard that they wore the fat off. When he remonstrated with one of the foremen about this, he only laughed and said that the stock would get the fat back again. The cattle-raisers had plenty of good fat horses, but they never learned anything. And—this must have irked Will—they had no chuck wagon; you had to tie your food to the saddle.

Will had two laughable encounters with Argentine methods of riding and roping, that have come down through posterity. On the Argentine ranches, the saddle ropes, some of which are sixty and seventy feet long, are fastened down on the side of the saddle, the ring being located on the girth instead of from a higher position on the saddle horn, as in America.

Consequently when Will dabbed his saddle on an

Argentine horse and roped a steer, the first yank of the steer jerked his horse off its feet, spilling Will. The horse had been trained to meet the shock from a much lower leverage, and hadn't been prepared for the higher pull.

Will next went out to show the Gauchos how to rope and tie down a steer. Seventeen years later he tells about it himself:

" . . . so I takes down my little manilla rope, and I even goes so far as to pick out about the exact bit of earth where I will lay this brute down. Well, I hadn't even got close enough to start swinging my rope when I heard something go whizzing over my head. A guy about twenty feet behind me had thrown clear over my head and caught the steer. I says to myself: 'I'll get fat showing these birds how to rope. They can rope an animal further than I could hit him with a rock'."

And now, before long, Will had no more money left. But his habit of reading the newspapers stood him in good stead. One day he read in a newspaper that a cargo of stock was to be shipped to South Africa, where Great Britain was busily occupied with the Boer War. At once Will applied for a job on the boat and got it.

On August 5, 1902, he sailed for Port Natal, on the eastern coast of Africa. He was on the move again!

Chapter 18
SOUTH AFRICA AND TEXAS JACK

WILL ROGERS was seasick every one of the thirty-two days of his trip to Africa. But this trip was different from the one he had made from England to South America, for then he was traveling first class while now he was working his way across and had to be on the job every day, in spite of his seasickness. It must have been a terrifically hard trip for him, but he did not complain of it in his letters home. Will had plenty of grit.

Shortly before he landed at Port Natal he narrowly missed being drowned at sea. He tells about it in a letter written September 22, 1902, from Mooi River, South Africa. Five ships which were only a day or so ahead of theirs went down with all on board. His own ship struck the tail end of the storm and barely escaped. Then while they were in the harbor unloading, one of the worst storms known for years wrecked sixteen sailing vessels right in the harbor, and filled it with sand and wreckage.

In the same letter he showed his flair for sizing up economic and labor conditions in a few terse sentences:

He advised all to fight shy of this country, unless they were skilled laborers. The common labor was done by Kaffirs or blacks, and "you have to see them to realize what wild-looking people they are." They traveled at a run all the time, and always singing. They were branded to show what tribe they belonged to. In Zululand he found the hardest layout of the lot.

Later he secured work at Mooi River and though he was working pretty hard, he says that he felt as fit as a racer. His principal job was to help feed and care for some thoroughbred horses and then take them out for an exercise gallop every day. That part would appeal to him, and we can see him in our imagination flying down the veldt, the wind in his nostrils, and perhaps waving an American hat in his exuberance at once more being on top of some good horse-flesh.

Some of the work, however, was not so good. It was helping the blacksmith put on shoes; "roaching mules and docking horses." When the boss would call, "Yank, bring out that horse," Will knew they meant him, and he would parade an animal before a prospective buyer, while the boss would be "a yellin' at me every minute."

One incident that particularly got Will's goat was some hurdle jumping. It was over a solid, four-foot stone wall. A mare that had been ridden only a time or two was put at this stiff hurdle and made to jump it. Will heard the melee and rushed out. As soon as the boss saw him, he yelled, "Yank, get on and ride her over." Will was taken by surprise, and although he had previously told the man that he didn't jump horses over hurdles, he saw that he would have to try. The worst of it was that the mare had neither saddle nor bridle—and here were "a lot of dagoes after it with whips and a solid, four-foot wall in front of you." But they took the wall all right, and Will kept after it until he could do it pretty well.

A letter from Will posted at Durban, Natal, South Africa, on November 17, 1902, disclosed that he had "shoved off from that 'Big Stuff' I have been with," and near Ladysmith had got a job breaking horses to be used by the British in the war. Several years later Will Rogers described the incident in an interview for the "New York Times":

"We had plenty to do, for many of the horses had never been ridden except by cowboys at inspection. You know a cowboy will ride sixty miles to see a fellow thrown from a horse. There's something so darned funny about it, you can't help laughing even if he gets hurt, but it is such a common sight over there we got so we wouldn't turn our heads. . . . American ponies killed more British soldiers than the Boers."

Meanwhile, back in Indian Territory, things were happening, too. The beautiful Cherokee country was fast being settled and towns were springing up along the railroad. More people were coming in all the time, occupying town sites, urging the platting of others, and starting banks and business houses. The old wild free life was no more.

That was one reason Will Rogers had left the land of his birth. He later told Herb McSpadden, his nephew, that he wasn't used to getting off his pony every few minutes to open a gate, or to working cattle in a fence corner.

Although Will did not know it, Charley McClellan, his closest friend during Willie Halsell days, had died. Charley's father had sent him to Cumberland University at Lebanon, Tennessee, in the hope that the boy would forget all his Indian foolishness. But Charley took his Indian outfit along with him and once, when William Jennings Bryan came to town to make a speech, Charley was asked to do an Indian war dance. He accepted eagerly and, donning his outfit, he made such a hit that Mr. Bryan personally congratulated him. "I am proud to meet a real American," he said.

At Cumberland Charley was popular and took part in all the student activities. He still wore his scalplock in a braid under his derby hat, and enjoyed the expression of surprise on the faces of the students and faculty when he took off the hat and let the long black braid tumble down. He soon became known as "Cherokee."

On Thanksgiving day, six months before he was to

be graduated, he was stricken with typhoid fever. His father and mother came and were with him when he died, December 24, 1902. By way of eulogy, the students at Cumberland got out a special memorial edition of the school newspaper paying tribute to him.

Will Rogers did not learn of his friend's death until several months later. At about the time Charley McClellan was taken ill, Will, in far-off Africa, made a six hundred mile trip to Johannesburg, to help ship a herd of horses.

When he got there he learned that there was a little American Wild-West show in town. Homesick for a sight of his own people, he determined to hunt up this show. He had money and a job, but with his old yearning for change, he was now ready for something new. Although he did not know it, Will Rogers was now standing at the threshold of his life's career.

Texas Jack was a smart American showman whose Wild West outfit often visited the British Army camps and was doing a thriving business. Will Rogers soon found the show and walked up to a lean, kindly-looking man who wore American boots and spurs. Will was so glad to see someone from home that he felt like crying. He was even glad to see the man's big hat.

"Howdy," the man said pleasantly, with a friendly Texas drawl, "I'm Texas Jack. What can I do for you?"

"I'm lookin' for a job," Will told him, a big grin

spreading over his face. "Got anything around here a feller might do?"

Texas Jack saw the boy was an American. He was interested.

"Wal, I might have," he said. "Who are you, son, and where do you hail from?"

"I'm Will Rogers from Indian Territory."

"Wal," said Texas Jack, still more interested, "if you come from Indian Territory, maybe you can ride and rope."

Will was disappointed. He could ride and rope all right, but not in a show. He wasn't an actor. He had expected to get a job driving tent pegs or working in the horse tent.

"I can ride and rope some," he admitted shyly, "only not good enough to do it in a show."

Texas Jack was studying him. Will mistook the silence for waning enthusiasm and hurried on lamely: "I guess I'm a little stronger on the ropin' than I am on the ridin'."

"Can you do tricks with a rope?"

"Oh——" Will ducked his head bashfully, looking alternately at Jack and the ground, "a few. But they don't amount to much."

A twinkle shone in Texas Jack's eyes. He stepped around the corner of the tent and came back with a rope, which he fed out as he walked. Will Rogers

THEN WILL DANCED IN AND OUT OF A VERTICAL SPIN

seemed fascinated with the rolling gait of the man and with the music of his big Mexican spurs—sights and sounds for which he was starved. Texas Jack had a pair of legs that bowed like inverted horse collars. He walked like some old cowman.

"Look here," said Jack and began to twirl the loop about him and pay it out in the giant spin known as the crinoline. Will moved back respectfully to give him room, and soon the rope was singing in the breeze. Finally Jack dropped it, gathered it in and proffered it to Will.

"Can you do that?" he asked.

Will showed no emotion as he accepted the rope, but his whole being leaped at the challenge. He began fooling with it. Soon it began to writhe and jump about like a charmed snake in the first stage of hypnotism. And then, suddenly, Will lifted it into the air and its convolutions became long and smooth and orderly, and Texas Jack saw his crinoline twirled as beautifully by the fluent wrist of this young stranger as he himself had ever twirled it in his life.

Then Will, moving almost shyly and apologetically, turned the full battery of his craft loose on Texas Jack. He danced in and out of horizontal spins, and the more difficult vertical ones. And though his repertoire then consisted of only a half dozen tricks, that was five more than Texas Jack could do. And Will Rogers could do them all well, thanks to the long hours he had practiced after seeing Oropeza at Chicago.

That was enough for Texas Jack. He hired Will then and there, and on December 15, 1902, Will wrote his father from Potchefstroon that Jack wanted him to do roping in the ring, but as the man who rode pitching horses was laid off, he had been doing this, too. They did a lot of plays showing Western life, and Will took the part of an Indian in some and of a Negro in others. He received twenty dollars a week and had a car to sleep in. The outfit consisted of about forty persons and thirty horses. "We generally stay in a town two or three days, and in the larger ones we have a crowded tent every night."

Will spoke in high terms of his employer, saying that Jack was the finest old boy he ever saw, and that he seemed to think a good deal of his young rider. Will thought that Jack was a better shot than Buffalo Bill, and a fine rider. He says also that the crowd of performers was "civilized," as Jack allowed no gambling or drinking.

Two weeks after Will started with Texas Jack, he sent his father $140, to pay for some insurance due; and the letter concluded with the significant statement that "I am going to learn things that will enable me to make my living in the world without making it by day labor."

This had become a grim resolve with him for, after several months of being on his own, Will Rogers was becoming steadier. At last he had found something he was to like and to stay with always—the show business. He was saving money and, better yet, sending it home. Experience was teaching him in a few short months what Clem Rogers, with all his good intentions and honest solicitation, had not been able to teach him in several years.

Will learned a great many things from Texas Jack. He studied his boss constantly and several years later he wrote:

"Jack was one of the smartest showmen I ever met. It was he who gave me the idea for my original stage act with my pony. I learned a lot about the show business from him. He could do a bum act with a rope, that an ordinary man couldn't get away with, and make the audience think it was great, so I used to study him by the hour and from him I learned the great secret of the show business—knowing when to get off. It's the fellow who knows when to quit that the audience wants more of."

Later he could not resist writing home describing his own proficiency. "I do all the roping," he says, "and am called 'The Cherokee Kid' on the program. Jack thinks I am ALL RIGHT and has raised my wages to $25 per week." He was already becoming a matinee hero, and the small boys would waylay him outside the tent to get him to show them how to rope.

Will soon became fond of roping zebras. It kept him busy, roping for Texas Jack at night and running zebras all day. Once he was chasing one down a slope when his horse stepped on a rolling stone, fell, and rolled over on him three or four times. Will was knocked out cleanly. He had a hole in the back of his head and the horse had both front legs broken. The horse had to be destroyed, but Will was a healthy boy and got well quickly.

In March he wrote his sisters from King's Hotel, East London, requesting special songs as he was taking the Negro part in one of Jack's plays, doing the cake walk and singing. He also wrote to Marshall Stevens, his old friend at Vinita, asking him to send him some silk Manilla yacht line ropes, and gave the measurements. Marshall was working in Lee Barrett's harness shop then and remembers that he sent the ropes to the American Consul at Cape Town, and that the foreign postage alone came to six dollars.

Will further amazed his father by sending him $310 from Port Elizabeth. "I'm getting homesick," he wrote, "but don't know now what I would do there, more than make a living." But he consoled himself with the thought that he was "worrying no one, and getting along first rate."

Will could have stayed on with Texas Jack and

probably, when Jack died a rich man a few years later, have inherited his fortune. For Jack had no relatives and was fond of Will. But, as usual, Will was anxious to be on the move, and so he quit the show and went to Australia. Jack gave him a letter to the Wirth brothers, who owned a big circus there, and he worked for them several months.

On November 29, 1903, in a letter from Marchison, Victoria, he gives a humorous account of his efforts with a boomerang: "The only way I could get it to come back," he says, "was to send one of the little black boys after it."

Will was beginning to develop shrewdness. Once, during a race meeting in Australia, he was astonishing the natives by hooking his toe around the saddle horn and, with his pony traveling at full speed, leaning backward until his head almost dragged in the sand and picking up three handkerchiefs with his hand.

An attendant came down and told him that the Governor-General, who was in the crowd, would like to see him do it again.

"All right," said Will, "tell him I'll do it again—for a hundred and fifty dollars."

Astounded, the attendant demured and protested.

"You tell the Governor-General that if he'll do it cheaper, I'll loan him my horse—and the handkerchiefs," grinned Will.

Although the Governor-General was not asked to put up the hundred and fifty dollars, a pot was made up and Will did the stunt again and pocketed the money. No wonder he was sending money home!

Will soon shipped for San Francisco, third class, and arrived home early in 1904. Later, he discussed that homecoming as follows:

"When I got back home I was so broke that some of the boys told Uncle Clem, 'Well, Willie got back from his trip around the world and he's wearing overalls for underpants'."

Chapter 19
THE MULHALL RANCH AND THE
WORLD'S FAIR OF 1904

COLONEL ZACK MULHALL, cattle baron of the nineties and livestock agent of the Frisco railroad, lived in a low-built, sprawling ranch house in the red lands of what had been the old Cherokee Strip. His ranch embraced nearly eight thousand acres, with a race track , stabling for a hundred horses, and room for unnumbered cattle. Here Colonel Mulhall lived grandly and boldly, entertaining many famous people at his table. Among them was Theodore Roosevelt, who was Zack's guest for two days during a western hunting trip and had the time of his life riding over Zack's vast domain and hunting jackrabbits and coyotes.

Colonel Mulhall had three daughters, Agnes, Lucille and Mildred; and one son, Charles, who became a champion cowboy and possessed his father's fondness of dabbling in Wild West shows and rodeos.

The Mulhall girls were raised on horseback and were all excellent riders. But the leading figure of this dashing group, who was eventually to become even better known than her father, was Lucille, a slim, strong, beautiful girl who spent all of her time with the horses and cattle. Her mother often protested that she would never learn any of the household arts if she spent all her time in the corral, but it did no good; Lucille was far more at home riding broncs and tying steers than she was in the kitchen.

At Fort Worth she once won a thousand dollar diamond medal for roping and tying a steer in the shortest time against all comers. At McAlester, Indian Territory, she once roped and tied three steers in thirty and a quarter, forty, and forty and four-fifths seconds respectively—amazing time. At Wichita, Kansas, her steer broke out of the arena, whereupon she put her horse over a five-foot fence, roped the runaway and tied and threw him one second and a half inside the record time.

Will's favorite at the Mulhall ranch was the kindly sweet-faced little mother of the group, Mrs. Mulhall. Having no mother of his own, Will all but adopted her, and when he was visiting at the Mulhall ranch he couldn't find enough ways to help her. He was always doing things for her—carrying water from the well, sweeping off the back porch, helping her feed the chickens, or gathering peach tree twigs from the orchard for her smoke house and building the smudge under the hanging meat to give it flavor. He would even put on an apron and help her in the kitchen.

Mrs. Mulhall was very fond of Will, too, and showed

it by baking him his favorite blackberry pie, a thing she seldom did for anyone else. "She would wrap the pie in oiled paper and hide it in the cupboard so that no one else would get it," her daughter Lucille remembers, "and if anybody else went near that cupboard, mother'd get real cranky."

In the Mulhall parlor after supper Will would follow her around like a pet puppy. Sometimes he'd sit on the floor and lay his head in her lap and she'd smile and fondle this straight black hair. Or if she were crocheting he'd hold the yarn for her on his hands.

"That's a big ball," he'd say, impatiently. "How much longer before you're gonna be through?"

"Well now, young man, it won't be very long," she'd reprove him, gently.

Sometimes when she was intent upon her sewing, he'd tease her by standing back six or eight feet and suddenly slipping a half-hitch over her foot with the white trick rope he always carried in his belt. Then he'd swiftly flip loop after loop over it until he had built a pile of snowy cord that completely hid her small shoe.

Other times he'd drop his rope around a picture of Lucille on the wall and exclaim in his mischievous drawl, "Ah! I got me a gal."

He roped everything on the place, dogs, calves, pigs, hats off the heads of the hands, anything that struck his whim. Lucille had several splendid greyhounds that followed her everywhere—Blue, Goo-goo, Queen, Troy and Jack—but when Will Rogers and his rope came on the place they'd all tuck their tails and run under the porch.

Once he even roped Tom, Mrs. Mulhall's brindle cat, around the stomach, and Tom squalled and spit like a terror until Will, laughing, petted him and eased the rope off him.

Agnes Mulhall, the eldest girl, had a fine musical education and her father had given her a grand piano for a graduation present. When Will visited the ranch he often induced Agnes to play and sing some of the songs he liked and, sitting beside her on the piano bench, he would sing lustily such songs as "I May Be Crazy But I Aint No Fool," one of his favorites.

Some years later Ring Lardner said of Will's voice that it had "something of the quality of that of a water spaniel with nightmare, but resembled more closely the mellow resonance of an Eighty-Fifth Street car making a turn on Madison Avenue." But no matter what was said about his voice, Will liked to sing, and Agnes Mulhall was always willing to play for him.

Sometimes he and Tom Mix, who was then just a cowboy and the drum major of Colonel Mulhall's Frisco Cowboy Band, would take Lucille and Mildred to dances. Their favorites were the Saturday night dances

held at the ranch home of John Offleger, who lived
seven miles from the Mulhall ranch. On those nights
Will would often stand on a chair or table and call the
dances. Lucille Mulhall remembers that two of his
favorite calls were:

> "Muley cow an' a white-face calf
> Swing your partner, once and a half."

And the other:

> "Down the center, cast off two,
> Big folks dance an' the little ones too."

Another visitor at the Mulhall ranch in those days
was a quiet fellow with the blackest hair anyone ever
saw and whose wide shoulders seemed much to heavy
for his slender body. He was Henry Starr, the notorious young Indian Territory outlaw who, like Will
Rogers, was part Cherokee.

Starr at that time had a five thousand dollar reward
over his head so he could not come freely to the Mulhall
ranch in the daytime, but had to slip in at night. The
coyote wail from the hills would long since be hushed
and the dark silent ranch buildings long asleep under
the blazing prairie stars, when Starr would ride up.
Cautiously, with his Indian instinct, he would move so
quietly that he would get within a few feet of the

sleeping Colonel's bedroom without even the dogs discovering him.

"Colonel! Colonel!" he would call from the brush in his low, evenly-modulated voice.

Mrs. Mulhall would hear him and rouse her husband. And the Colonel, who had known and liked Starr's father and mother in the old days, would let him in and hide him in the attic where Starr would sleep away much of the following day.

Late in the afternoon he would venture downstairs and curling up in a corner with his feet tucked under him, he would play solitaire or read, apparently oblivious of everything around him. He was so quiet that you would have to look at him twice to see that he was there, but if Mrs. Mulhall dropped her ball of yarn, Starr, moving with all the lithe grace of a cat and just as silently, would deftly pick it up and hand it to her with a quiet smile. Or if a horse approached from the road, Starr's nostrils would distend and his black eyes become stationary. He always heard hoofbeats long before anyone else.

The young outlaw loved vanilla ice cream. At dusk, when supper was over, he would say to little Mildred Mulhall: "Well, isn't it about our ice cream time?" They would drive down town, where Starr would give her the money and wait in the buggy while Mildred went in and bought a quart of the frozen delicacy. The little girl never knew why they always went at night.

Occasionally Colonel Zack, who loved good shooting, would take Starr out into the pasture and spin quarters into the air just to see him shoot them down. Starr who was a marvelous shot with a Winchester, could hit three out of five. Shooting was a gift with him.

This young outlaw, unlike other bandits, would never shoot into a crowd of townspeople. But he once killed a man in a duel and was captured and sentenced to twenty-five years in the penitentiary. He served five years of his term and was then pardoned by President Roosevelt.

At the time of the World's Fair in St. Louis, in 1904, Colonel Mulhall was taking up a bunch of crack ropers and riders and asked Starr to go along. The colonel wanted to help him to go straight, and planned to take him to St. Louis and set him up in business.

Will Rogers, just back from his trip around the world, went too, joining the Cummings Indian Congress and doing special roping for Colonel Mulhall at the Delmar Gardens on Sunday.

When they arrived at St. Louis, Will worked very hard. While the rest of the cowpunchers were still in bed, he would be up before daylight, practicing loops and spins with his rope on the show lot.

"He was always working with a rope," recalls Jim Minnick, then a young Texas horse-trainer who shared his room with Will at St. Louis. "He was tireless. He even practiced right in our room, looking into a mirror and lassoing the bed post over his shoulder. Will could do anything with a rope except throw it up in the air and climb it."

Will would work seven days in the week if he could.

LUCILLE MULHALL, WORLD'S GREATEST COWGIRL
(Photo courtesy of Moppy Fisch, Lucille Mulhall's neice)

He did trick roping at both matinee and evening performances in Charley Tompkins's little Wild West show, and on Sunday he and Jim worked for Colonel Mulhall at Delmar Gardens.

Tompkins owned the famous Golding string of bucking horses, the toughest in the world at that time. He had sixty-five horses, twenty-five cowboys and eight girls. Among the men were Thad Sowders, the world's champion bronc rider, who had won the diamond belt at the Mountain and Plains festival at Denver in 1902 and 1903; Otis and Curtis Jackson, a pair of hard-twisted youngsters from Nebraska; Sam Scovill, later a world champion, and Frank Still, a bucking horse rider from Geary, Oklahoma.

"Will did trick roping for me," Charley Tompkins related many years later. "He was a good bronc rider but we didn't need him. He spun butterflies, and jumped through his loop and caught running horses by the feet, calling his catches. But before he'd try one, he'd face the crowd and drawl:

"'Now folks, I'm gonna try to jump through the rope and catch the hoss by the forefeet.' He'd close the act by jumping in the saddle, riding Comanche around the hippodrome ring and then doing the big loop around both his horse and himself."

But he had one trick he would not show at St. Louis. No one had ever seen anything like it anywhere, and he did not want to do it for the sixty dollars a month he was getting there, but was saving it for the time when he would get better pay.

Will had got the idea for this trick from Texas Jack in South Africa, and at St. Louis he and Jim Minnick would go out to a pasture four miles from the fair grounds and practice it in secret.

When Will first showed Jim the new trick, the latter was amazed to see Will take his place on the ground and shake out two ropes, holding one in his left hand and the other in his right.

"Gosh, Will, what's the idea of the two ropes?" Jim asked.

Will Rogers grinned mysteriously. "Ride your horse by me and I'll show you," he invited.

Jim did, and as he sped past, Will threw both ropes almost simultaneously. The one in his left hand dropped around the horse's neck and the one in his right dropped around Jim's neck. And Jim himself was so astonished at this clever trick that he almost dropped out of his saddle.

After a little while Will Rogers picked up a third job in St. Louis, and this job marked the first stage appearance of his life. Ted McSpadden, a relative of Will's and a crack roper himself, was offered a chance to do trick roping during the intermission at a burlesque show in the old Standard theater in St. Louis. Ted

asked Will Rogers to help him and Will accepted eagerly. It was a twenty minute act in which they did
spinning, butterflies, and roped each other. There are
old times who say that Ted McSpadden was at that
time a better roper than Will, and Will himself once
told Jim Rider: "Teddy can see and do a new trick in ten
minutes, where it'd take me a week."

Although Will was not making a great deal of money,
he was not spending much either, and was behaving
more sensibly than he ever had before. He did not
drink or smoke or chew tobacco—instead, he chewed
gum. And he read every newspaper he could lay his
hands on.

Jack Wright, a cowboy who met Will at St. Louis,
pays him a fine tribute. "The atmosphere around Will
was always friendly," he says. "He fit into any setting,
whether high or low, and always seemed at home,
whether among the Indians in their improvised camps
around the fair grounds, or sitting on a wagon tongue
with the gypsies. He loved children—Indian, gypsy,
black or white—above everything else, and was often
discovered at the Indian camp on the rodeo grounds,
squatted on the ground, Indian fashion, telling tales to
the children gathered around him.

"Although he was a little careless about his personal
appearance, he was spotless in body and mind, kind-
hearted, generous, forgiving and gentle-mannered."

While Will Rogers was busy doing his roping in the three shows for which he was working, Henry Starr had also gone to work in St. Louis. Colonel Zack Mulhall had got him to change his name, had given him new clothes and a good job. Starr did well for a time and made friends easily.

But one morning when he and Colonel Mulhall were walking down Broadway, Starr spied a bank on a prominent corner and his black eyes kindled exultantly.

"Say, look at that bank!" he exclaimed, "sittin' there right on that corner. It'd be a cinch—"

"Hold on there, son," Colonel Mulhall warned, looking at him aghast, "you've done fine here so far. I'd shore hate to see you spoil it all by holdin' up a bank!"

But three weeks later a Webster Groves bank was held up and robbed and Starr was gone. Later he robbed a bank in Colorado, was sentenced and pardoned. Then he held up two banks in Stroud, Oklahoma, was shot, captured, sentenced and pardoned for the third time.

But his love of excitement would not let him go straight. He robbed a bank at Harrison, Arkansas, and was shot and killed.

Back at the Colonel's ranch, Mrs. Mulhall cried when she heard about it, for Henry Starr was one of her "boys" and she like him just as she did Will Rogers.

Chapter 20
MADISON SQUARE GARDEN AND
VAUDEVILLE

IN APRIL, 1905, Colonel Zack Mulhall secured the
Wild West concession at the annual Horse Show in
Madison Square Garden, New York City, and Will
Rogers went along as a roper, and for the first time
revealed his two-rope trick. But the real star of the
show was Lucille Mulhall, who with her sisters, Mildred and Agnes, and a fourth girl, Georgia Taylor,
amazed the Easterners with exhibitions of horse-
manship.

The colonel had assembled the best riders and ropers
anywhere. Besides Tom Mix, who did bulldogging and
bronc-riding, there were Jack Joyce, pony express
rider and "bronch buster," Otto Kline, the champion
trick rider of the world, Colonel Toops, who did straight
riding and announcing, George Elser, trick rider,
Chester Byers, boy roper, Otis and Curtis Jackson,
"bronch-busters," Zack Miller, Harry Shanton, Charley
Mulhall and Jim Minnick.

"Will's act was much smoother and better than it
was at St. Louis," Charley Mulhall said later. "When
they'd announce him, he'd hook his heel around the

saddle horn of his running horse, lean over backward with his head nearly touching the ground, and come in draggin' his hand in the sand. Then he'd dismount and we'd run horses past him and he'd yell like a Comanche and roping from the ground, jump through his loop backwards and catch 'em by any foot and even their tail. He also did a graceful dance over the spinning rope to band music, and dropped a big loop over six or seven horses running in a group. The climax of this act was his two-rope trick, then he'd ride around the arena spinning the big loop, ride to the center, take off his hat, let out a yell and ride out."

Colonel Mulhall was a thorough believer in showmanship. In the grand entry he would come in last, riding Jim Bellew, a big brown horse named for the foreman of his ranch. They made an imposing pair. Old Jim Bellew would come in on a dead run, then suddenly pull up and slide five or six feet in the gravel, rear up on his hind feet and snort. The colonel would sweep off his big hat and bow.

All the boys liked the colonel because he would dress them up and take them everywhere. But money ran through his hands, and he could not always pay regularly. When he had plenty of money, he paid big wages, but when he was broke so were his cowboys.

Jim Minnick tells a story that illustrates the generosity of Colonel Mulhall. "Once I heard that Colonel

COLONEL ZACK MULHALL, BOSS OF THE MADISON
SQUARE GARDEN SHOW

Zack had a big roll and was treating everybody at the bar of the Fifth Avenue Hotel," Jim says. "He did this because it was good advertising for the show. I slipped up in the crowd and watched him and pretty soon I saw him flash a big roll with a one hundred dollar bill on the outside. I stepped up. 'Colonel, I need some money to get my horses shod.' He never hesitated, but shucked off that hundred dollar bill and handed it to me. I ran and told Will Rogers and Will hot-footed it to the colonel. But he wasn't as lucky as I was—he only got twenty dollars."

A few days later there occurred an incident that put Will Rogers's name in all the New York papers. During the afternoon performance before six thousand people at Madison Square Garden, a steer was cut out for Lucille Mulhall to rope. He was a big mouse-colored, long-horned Texas brute, and the first thing he did was to jump over three wooden bars that closed the entrance to a tier of boxes.

"Whoof!" he bellowed, and stood there sniffing and pawing the wooden floor and looking around at the people. But in another minute he went into action. With a bellow of fun he threw up his tail, vaulted into the lower boxes and, climbing like a mountain goat, he scrambled up into the second balcony toward the band. The spectators fled, screaming, and the music broke off discordantly, and the bandsmen, throwing their instruments to right and left, ran for their lives.

Five cowboys, Will Rogers and Tom Mix among them, ran after the animal. A blue clad policeman sprinted just ahead of Will, and Will called to him jocularly as he ran: "Hey, Policeman, what are you gonna do with that steer when you catch him?"

Suddenly the bull turned, and splintering the seats in front of him, made for the policeman. Now the situation was reversed and the bull was chasing the policeman! The big garden was a bedlam of mingled roars and screams.

With his genius for being remarkably keen-witted in a crisis, Will Rogers, who always had a rope in his hands, quickly shook it out. As the steer ran past him Will dabbed the rope around its neck and, snubbing it around a steel post and throwing his weight on the rope, he checked the animal's headlong flight. With the help of the other cowboys Will led the steer back down into the arena, while the scared crowd cheered him to the echo.

This incident proved valuable to Will Rogers. Before it happened he had been quietly working up a new act, one that would fit the stage of the average theater, which is smaller than the arena of a Wild West show. Will had never roped a horse in so small a space, but he patiently went to work and marked off the dimensions of a stage on the ground. Then for two months he and

Jim Minnick practiced there in secret. Later they practiced their act indoors. Although Comanche weighed only nine hundred and fifty pounds, he was too big for the new act and Will had to use Teddy, a small tame bay horse that Mrs. Mulhall had given him.

Thanks to the publicity attending the roping of the stampeding bull, a great many people now knew who Will Rogers was, and Will decided his opportunity had arrived. Calling on an agency, he tried to sell his act. But the booking agents were not sure. Nobody had ever seen a man rope a horse on a stage before. But Will kept after them relentlessly. One of them offered him a trial at seventy dollars a week, but with typical horse-trading shrewdness, he held out for two hundred and fifty dollars.

At last, because Will gave them no peace, an agency agreed to put him on at his own terms. Two hundred and fifty dollars a week was a good sum of money, but it was not too much, for Will had to pay a helper, feed the horse, pay for its transportation and pay all his own expenses besides.

His first appearance was in the old Fourteenth Street Union Square Theater in New York City and Jim Minnick, who rode Will's horse for the roping act, told of the experience later.

"Will wasn't a bit nervous," he said. "He was keen for the act to begin. We buckled rubber boots on Teddy and took him up the stairs to the theater. That little old horse could have climbed a ladder. As I rode Teddy past Will, he'd rope the horse by one, two, three, or all four feet, and also by his tail. Teddy would always slow up when he felt the loop around his feet. 'Now folks,' Will would say, 'this is a pretty good stunt—if I can do it.' Then he'd purposely rope the pony by three feet, saying: 'Got 'em all but one that time.' The next time he'd get all four feet, and the crowd would cheer madly. They didn't appreciate that it was harder to rope a horse by three feet than by all four."

Jim was too busy looking after his polo ponies to stay long with Will and after a week Will got a boy to help him, and later he got Buck McKee of Pawnee, Oklahoma, who had been a deputy marshal and had come east with Pawnee Bill's circus.

Back at the Bank of Claremore, President Jim Hall and Vice-President Clem Rogers did not like Will's new business. In those days the show business was considered wild and disgraceful.

"Jim," said Clem, "I'm awful blue. Will's going into the show business. What would you do about it?"

"Well, Clem," replied Hall, "I'd just knock him in the head, because he'll never amount to anything!"

Clem Rogers sighed. "I'm afraid you're right," he said.

But in spite of his father's misgivings, Will's act

prospered. He first roped as an extra at a supper show, between the hours of six and eight in the evening when the crowds were slim. But soon the novelty of his act made it more popular.

And then one afternoon Willie Hammerstein saw him, and put him on the Victoria roof. Will later spoke of this in an interview for the New York *Times*. "I didn't want to go at first, because the stage was so small," he said, "But he (Hammerstein) said the smallness of the stage would make the act. There was a great showman— Willie Hammerstein. He was right about my act. They thought it was wonderful I could do stunts with my pony in so small a space, and I stayed on the roof all summer."

Soon Will began sending money home to Clem to invest for him. At first Clem was afraid Will hadn't got the money honestly, but he soon found out differently and was forced to change his estimate of his son's new profession.

At this time Will did not talk to his audiences as he did later in his stage career. But he often talked to Buck McKee while doing his roping.

"He would come out and do his tricks without saying much unless the trick failed," Buck told of him, "then he'd crack some joke and I'd laugh from the wings."

At last the manager urged Will to talk to the audiences as he did to Buck. For a time Will refused but

WILL BEGAN TALKING INFORMALLY TO THE AUDIENCE

after a while he decided to try an announcement. He thought it might help the crowd to understand what he was trying to do.

He came out onto the stage one evening, chewing gum as usual, stopped the orchestra and, without any rehearsing, began talking informally to the audience:

"Ladies and gentlemen," he said, "I want to call your sho'nuff attention to this next little stunt I am going to pull on you, as I am going to throw about two or three ropes at once, catching the horse with one and the rider with the other. I don't have any idea I'll get it, but here goes."

To his surprise and chagrin the audience laughed at him. They laughed uproariously, and Will was hurt and angry. He thought they were making fun of him. "They laughed so much I thought they were boobing me, and I wouldn't do it again for weeks," he explained later. "But it was the luckiest thing I ever did. I can't claim credit for it. It took all my friends to drive me to it."

When he again began to talk to his audiences it was mostly in droll explanation of his stunts. He found the best outlet for his quips in his "misses," and since he seldom missed, he finally took to missing on purpose.

"Shoot!" he would say, drawing in his rope and pretending displeasure, "I wish the management of this here theater would let a feller cuss!" And this drew a perfect tornado of laughter.

Once when a rope got tangled up with his legs he looked up bashfully and said: "Wal, I'd a dawgoned sight rather have it aroun' my laigs than aroun' my neck." And again the crowd laughed. There was something sunny and different about this young cowboy whose pungent wit was as refreshing as a draught of fresh air off his prairie.

Gradually the laughter encouraged him. He saw that it was sincere and that people were laughing because they really enjoyed him. So he began to try to make them laugh more.

Once he appeared loaded down with enough musical instruments to equip a symphony, and laid them on a table on the stage. Then he took out his rope, did his stunts, picked up the instruments and walked out. And the people, who'd been waiting all through the act for him to play the banjo, the violin and other instruments, always laughed.

He had a trick of standing upstage during his act, and suddenly tossing his rope back of him into the wings and dragging out an actor or a theater manager who had been standing there, unseen by the audience, watching his act. Or at other times, when he himself would be standing in the wings watching some act, he would wait until a fellow actor was about to take a bow and then, out of sight of the crowd, catch him with a rope and drag him off the stage.

Although he worked fifty weeks each year, Will occasionally went home to see his father and sisters. He was becoming more and more interested in Betty Blake. She was a sweet, sensible girl and Will liked her very much. Once when he was at home, his sister Maud gave him a house party at Chelsea and invited Betty who was visiting there also. Sallie, his oldest sister, gave a dinner as did Mary Strange, a friend, and there were other parties as well. Betty stayed a week and Will saw much of her during that time.

Meanwhile he had made a trip to Europe at the request of Steinert, a famous German producer who had liked his act in America. He was quite a hit in Berlin, although once his fondness for roping someone in the wings and dragging them onto the stage almost got him into trouble. On this occasion he lassoed a fireman who stood there on duty with an ax, and almost caused a panic!

Later he and Shea, his booking agent, went on to London where Will tried to secure an engagement with the London producer, Budd. But Budd would have nothing to do with the act. Finally Will offered to play a day or two for nothing with the understanding that if his act was successful he would be engaged for a week. Budd agreed to this and the act was so well received that it continued for three weeks.

BUCK MCKEE AND PONY TEDDY

One day Will received a visit from an official asking him to appear at the King's club. Urged by Shea, he went and made a great hit with Edward VII, who presented him with a tall loving cup.

Will was always helping people. His generosity was boundless, and no one in trouble ever appealed to him in vain. In fact he was so eager to be of service to his friends that often they had difficulty in refusing his proffers of money. Once, when he read that the McCaddon circus was stranded in Europe and its actors were returning to America, he looked up two of them, Charley and Mable Tompkins, who were friends of his. A few hours after they landed from Europe, Will confronted them suspiciously.

"How'd you get back—swim?" he asked.

Charley Tompkins foresaw Will's good intentions and although he and Mable had only nine dollars between them, he knew that Will Rogers was helping a dozen other jobless actors, and did not want to impose on his generosity.

"We came back on the boat, first class," Charley lied cheerfully.

But Will Rogers was hard to fool. "Now look here," he insisted, "I'm workin', you know. How're you fixed? Got anything to eat on?"

"Sure, Will," said Charley, "we're all right. We'll get along."

Will was still suspicious and followed them around for two or three days, trying to persuade them to let him help, but they wouldn't.

But another time when Will insisted on helping, they allowed him to, and the story of that incident is the story of one of the finest charities of Will Rogers' life.

Lottie Lynch was a circus girl, the wife of Joe Lynch, a cowboy actor. She had contracted tuberculosis in New York, and her husband was hundreds of miles away in St. Louis, broke. The girl was helplessly ill, and naturally wanted to see her husband before she died.

Charley and Mabel Tompkins, then out of work themselves, tried to help her. They moved her to Lebanon Hospital and later to their own apartment in the Bronx. But Lottie was sinking fast.

One day Will Rogers happened to visit the Tompkins and learning of the girl's plight he told them he was going to send her to her husband.

"Now Will," protested Charley, "you don't have to do this. Mabel and I will soon be fixed so we can send her."

But Will ducked his head and shook it in the shy but decisive way that indicated that his mind was made up.

"Nawp, Nawp," he said quietly but firmly, "I owe this to my friends. Joe's a good old boy."

Not only did he pay Lottie Lynch's hospital bill at Lebanon, but he also bought her a stateroom to St. Louis and gave her enough money to take care of her after she got there.

Lottie did not live long. Soon a telegram came from Joe Lynch announcing her death. But Will Rogers and the Tompkins had made her last weeks as pleasant as possible.

Chapter 21
MARRIAGE

BETTER THAN anything else, Will Rogers liked to see his old cowboy friends when they occasionally drifted east and looked him up.

Once when he came out on the stage in an eastern city, somebody let out a cowboy yell from back in the audience. Instantly Will's eyes lit up and he craned his neck over the footlights.

"I hear an Indian Territory whoop," he called. "Stand up out there whoever you are."

A grinning, leather-faced fellow stood up, back in the theater. It was Charley Walker, whom Will had known at Vinita in his Willie Halsell days.

"Why, hello there, Charley," Will called, forgetting all about the rest of the audience, "meet me back stage after the show."

One day in 1906, Will's search for a friend resulted in a chance meeting with Fred Stone, then a young actor, and out of this meeting grew a life-long friendship. Will had gone to the Knickerbocker Hotel, in New York City, to find Evans Chambers, an expert roper from Claremore, Oklahoma, who answered to the name

214

of "Blackie," but was told by Fred Stone that Blackie had gone back home because of sickness.

Fred Stone had to learn a lariat dance to use in a play, and not knowing how to rope, he had asked Blackie to teach him. But now with Blackie gone, Fred would have to look around for another teacher.

"Say, I'm a roper," Will told him shyly. "What was Blackie teaching you? Trick ropin'?"

Fred explained to him about the lariat dance. "Shucks!" Will exclaimed, "ropin' ain't hard. I can teach you all the ropin' you want to know."

Stone invited him to the theater and Will kept his word. He not only taught Fred the rope dance, but came back often to teach him other roping tricks. Soon they were fast friends and Will had found a pal who would be close to him all his life.

In November, 1908, Will made a quick trip to Rogers, Arkansas, a trip that could have but one ending—his marriage. He had loved Betty Blake deeply for a long time and they had often talked of marriage, but not until recently had Will been able to persuade Betty that an early marriage was practical. It is easy to understand her hesitation, for Will was just starting in vaudeville with an unique act that might lose its popularity at any time.

But at present it was going well and the audiences were liking it better and better, so at last Betty gave

MR. AND MRS. WILL ROGERS

her consent and their wedding took place at the home of her mother, Mrs. A. J. Blake.

And now Will kept grinding away at his act. Each week he talked a little more, and gradually gained experience and poise. Not all of his quips brought laughs, but when they did not, he knew what to do. "Then I got busy and gave the audience two minutes of the darndest rope swingin' you ever saw," he explained.

Will always liked seeing Wild West shows come to town. They never lost their glamor for him. In early December of 1908, Pawnee Bill, who had acquired the controlling interest in the Buffalo Bill Wild West show, brought it to New York City. Although Will Rogers was working in a midnight show, he was on the grounds waiting for the cowboys, when Pawnee Bill's baggage wagons arrived.

At breakfast in the big mess tent that morning, Will sat at the head of the long table and kept the cow-punchers guffawing at his yarns. He got a great pleasure out of seeing his old buddies again, and also out of the meal itself, for Pawnee Bill always "fed good," as his actors said.

Pawnee Bill later told of that time. "Our opening night was a gala affair," he said. "Buffalo Bill himself was there with General Nelson A. Miles and other army officers, in General Miles's box. In my box I had Boss Murphy of Tammany Hall and also the Governor and the Mayor.

"I hadn't realized that Will Rogers was getting somewhere in the show game until I heard him introduced that night. His ovation astounded me. It was greater than anybody's except Buffalo Bill's, and almost as great as his. And how the crowd loved to see him rope!

"I had sent a man to Mexico City to hire the finest vaqueros available for my show, but Will Rogers was more popular than all of them put together. The crowd had eyes only for him.

"After the show I encountered Will at the dressing room door. I tried to pay him.

"'Shucks, Major,' he laughed bashfully, 'you don't have to pay me. I'm havin' too good a time here. I ought to be payin' you. All I want is the right to go to your grub tent. I can't get eatin' like that anywhere else in New York'."

However Pawnee Bill made Will finally take sixty dollars a week for his work.

Pawnee Bill also recalled that Will was not the least jealous of other great ropers. He loved roping so well that he could even enjoy seeing a rival do it.

"Once Will was standing near me during the show," he said. "We were watching my Mexican vaqueros do their marvelous roping.

"'Major,' said Will, 'did you notice that little Mexi-

can on the east side of the Garden? Why, if I could rope
like that little fellow, the Lord only knows how high I
could go. These Mexicans begin ropin' where we leave
off'."

In 1910 Will got the idea that he wanted to organize
a show of his own, a big ten-horse vaudeville act. He
collected some of the best riding talent available and
began rehearsing at Bayonne, New Jersey. But the act
never got away from Bayonne. It was too big and
unwieldy.

"Well," Will said one day, "we can't make her go.
Guess we'll quit." And he paid off, giving everyone an
extra week's pay, although he had lost money on the
act and didn't have much to start with. He was a good
loser. And not only a good loser but an honest one.

Whenever their booking permitted, Will and Betty
visited back home. They would spend time both at
Rogers, Arkansas, where Betty's people lived, and at
Chelsea, with Will's father and sisters.

Clem Rogers was still vigorous in spite of his seventy
years. Mary Bibles, his second wife, had died in 1900,
and Clem had taken a suite of rooms over the First
National Bank at Claremore, where he lived alone.

Beside all the other honors that had been paid him,
another and a lasting one had come to him. In 1907 the
Indian Territory country had been combined, with the
western lands adjoining it, into the new state of

Oklahoma. When the counties were formed, the one
that included the land adjacent to Claremore, Oologah
and Chelsea was named Rogers County, in honor of
Clem, who was a member of the new state's first
constitutional convention. Will was very proud of this
honor paid to his father and in one of his later talks he
said:

"Dear old devoted Father! Rogers County was named
for him. Papa was an old convention man. He swung
along with most of the others on their pet schemes, but
when it came time to divide the state into counties, he
struck out for himself. He knew that country perfectly.
He'd go up a river, see a creek and go up it until soon
he had every acre of good soil in that county. They had
to stop him once before he could cross the border into
Arkansas. When he finally got through, Rogers County
looked like a tarantula."

Clem punctually spent his weekends at Chelsea.
Each Saturday night he would take the Frisco to
Chelsea where his daughter, Maud, would meet him
and have a hot supper waiting for him. After going to
church on Sunday, he would return to Maud's for
dinner, and then go to the house of his oldest daughter,
Sallie, where he would spend Sunday night. After
eating at Sallie's Monday noon, he'd return to
Claremore on the train.

He like this program because it permitted him to

have dinner and supper and spend one night at the home of each of his daughters.

One morning in October, 1911, Clem got a telegram from Will announcing the birth of a son, Will, Jr. He was greatly pleased at this and, naturally, he was anxious to see his new grandson.

But he was never to see this first child born to Will and Betty. Just two weeks later, Clem went to Chelsea as usual and, following his custom, he had supper at the home of his daughter, Maud. After an evening of pleasant visiting, he retired at nine o'clock, feeling fine. But when they called him for breakfast the next morning, there was no answer, although he was an early riser.

When breakfast was ready Clem still had not made his appearance, so Estelle Lane, Maud's oldest daughter, was sent to waken him. Her cries summoned the family. Clem Rogers apparently had died quickly of a heart attack in the night.

Will was telegraphed to and arrived the following Tuesday morning for the funeral. All the business houses in Claremore were closed and special trains were run to Chelsea for that sad event.

Will Rogers felt the death of his father keenly. Clem had always been very good to him and Will had loved and admired him greatly.

Chapter 22
FAME

WHEN HE began to put into words his observations on the human scene, Will Rogers, the roper, became Will Rogers, the beloved American humorist.

There are several reasons why his patter became nationally popular. One is its brevity. He could usually make his point in a sentence or two. Also, there is the fact that what he said was based on truth.

"Personally I don't like jokes that get the biggest laugh," he once said to an interviewer for the "American Magazine," "I like one, where, if you are with a friend and you hear it, it makes you think, an' you nudge your friend an' say: 'He's right about that.' I would rather have you do that than to laugh—and then forget the next minute what you laughed at."

Later he developed the habit of punning about timely topics, and he had an ace reporter's instinct for news value. "A joke don't have to be near as funny if it's up-to-date," he once said. Always he was himself, and whatever he told was twice as good when flavored with the pungency of his own personality.

"I see the President made another speech the other day," he would drawl, hopping in and out of the whistling circle of his rope and chewing his gum vigorously. "I reckon some guy will come along and misunderstand him. It must be awful hard for a smart man like the President to make a speech in such a way that the bonehead and the highbrow will both get what he means."

Will always was a tremendous worker and now, slowly but surely, he was making a name for himself. After five years he abandoned the act with Buck McKee and pony Teddy, and became a trick-roping monologist who rarely repeated a gag, and who made up his act as he went along.

In 1914 he was signed by Florenz Ziegfeld, a producer who was giving America glorious entertainment with his Follies and his Night Frolics. When Will first went with Ziegfeld he got one hundred and twenty-five dollars a week for the season. By this third year he was making three hundred and fifty dollars, and two years later he had been raised to six hundred dollars.

"What's the idea?" Ziegfeld once asked, when Will asked for a raise, "last year you told me your wife and children would be satisfied with four hundred a week."

"They were," Will told him, "but since then I've got another child and he's kicking."

Eddie Cantor, who with W. C. Fields and Bert Wil-

liams, the great colored entertainer, was in the Follies
with Rogers, remembers him first as "out of place," a
lonely cowboy struggling along with a bunch of hoofers
and wise-crackers.

But soon Will got better acquainted. He knew everybody, and developed the habit of spotting important
men and women in the audience, roping them and
asking them to come to the stage and speak briefly.
Shortly after W. G. McAdoo was defeated for the
Democratic nomination for the Presidency, he appeared
in one of Will's audiences and Will coaxed him up to
the stage.

"I thought I was out of politics," Mr. McAdoo began.

"You are!" interrupted Will, and the house roared.

Will's popularity was growing steadily. Audiences
knew him and watched for him. As his reputation and
his confidence grew, he began poking fun at Presidents
of the United States. Woodrow Wilson was the first
president he played before after he began joking about
national affairs from the stage. Rogers was in Baltimore
at the time, where his act was sponsored by the Friars'
Club, a theatrical organization of New York, and
President Wilson had come over from Washington to
see the show.

Will was nervous. He was about to attempt something
brand new in theatrical work—he was going to poke
fun at a president of the United States—with the

President in the audience. He was not at all sure how the President would take it.

After warming up with one or two general quips, Rogers tried his first shot at President Wilson. At that time General Pershing was leading an American invasion into Mexico after the bandit Villa, and the papers were full of it, so it was of this that Will spoke.

"I see where they have captured Villa," he said with a grin. "Yep, they got him in the morning editions but the afternoon ones let him get away."

The crowd, eager to laugh, waited to see how President Wilson would take it, and after a moment it grew so quiet that the only sound Will could hear was the hiss of his spinning rope. Then the President burst out laughing and everybody followed.

From then on, Will was off in characteristic fashion on both the Mexican and European situations, with President Wilson leading the audience in laughter at the jokes on himself.

"I see by a headline that 'Villa escapes net and flees'," went on Will. "Any Mexican that can escape fleas, is beyond catching!"

It probably was Will Rogers's proudest moment when, after the show was over, the President came back stage to meet the cast and personally congratulated him.

Will was always grateful to President Wilson for

being such a good sport. "You can always tell a big man from a little one;" he said afterward, "the big ones don't get sore when you joke about them."

At the insistence of Mr. and Mrs. Rex Beach, whom he met through Fred Stone, Will Rogers, then thirty-nine years old, began to make silent pictures in 1919. His first picture was "Laughing Bill Hyde," and Will made it one summer back east, without losing one moment from his duties with the Follies.

From 1919 to 1922 he devoted all his time to making silent pictures. They were mostly one and two reel pictures on both serious and comical subjects. He also made a series of shorts for Pathe, entitled "Strolling Thru Europe with Will Rogers." Some of the better known titles were: "The Texas Steer," "Honest Hutch," "Family Fits," "Jes' Call Me Jim," "Boys Will Be Boys," "Doubling for Romeo," "Two Wagons, Both Covered," "Jubilo, Jr.," "Our Congressman," and "Gee Whiz, Genevieve."

Although his silent pictures never were as successful as his later talking pictures, because there was then no way of recording his Indian Territory drawl, the screen caught part of his personality, and he was moderately successful, giving several fine character performances. One of the best of these was that of "Tennessee's Partner," in the film version of Bret Harte's wistful short story. Will took the part of the faithful, simple fellow who remained the loyal friend of the gambler although the latter stole his wife.

But the silent picture that Will's old buddies back on the ranches like best was "The Ropin' Fool." In this picture Will had plenty of opportunity to do all kinds of roping, and he did them well. Jim Rider saw the picture in 1924 at Nowata, Oklahoma, and enjoyed watching his old friend on the screen.

"Will really roped in that picture," he said. "He was workin' on a ranch. There was a girl in the deal. The boss was nutty about the girl. Without half tryin' Will was beatin' his time. The boss didn't like it.

"One day Will rode over the hill and jumped some big steers. He went to hog-tyin' 'em just for fun. He got pretty tired. After he'd hog-tied one and sat down to rest, the boss rode up. It was just the chance he'd been waitin' for. 'You know we don't allow the hands to contest these cattle,' he said. 'You're fired.'

"Will looked up the slope where about twenty-five goats were grazin', and said: 'That contestin' rule don't include goats, does it?' and went up and roped goats. He tied down half a dozen.

"He quit ranchin' but he couldn't quit ropin'. Further on in the picture there was a coach horse standin' tied. He was a hackney and had a little six-inch tail. Will decided to have some fun and rope that stub tail, but every time his rope would hit the horse on the hip, the horse would clamp his tail down and the rope would slip off. Will was puzzled. He walked off an' scratched his head. Then he grinned. With his back to the horse, he spun his rope, jumped through the loop, whirled around and dabbed the rope so tight on the root of that stub tail that if fitted like a crupper. Of course he'd been stallin' all the time.

"Another place he was in bed asleep. A wood rat got to gnawin' in the room. He woke Will up. Will yawned, laid the covers back, reached up at the head of the bed and got a little short tie-rope about four feet long, roped that wood rat around the neck, tied him to the bed post and climbed back in bed and went to sleep with the little wood rat buckin' around there like a broncho.

"Will also did a three-rope stunt in that picture. A man came by him full speed on a horse. Will caught the horse by the front feet with the first loop, around the neck with the second, an' then picked up the third and nailed the rider.

"He used the Johnny Blocker throw I'd learned him. So I wrote him in New York and told him: 'Will, you shore upset that Johnny loop purty!' He wrote back: 'Jim, we had an awful time findin' an old work ox gentle enough for me to rope!'"

Will Rogers tried his hand as an author in 1919, and wrote two books, both published by Harpers, "The

Cowboy Philosopher on the Peace Conference" and "The Cowboy Philosopher on Prohibition." Although neither had a very wide circulation, selling approximately five thousand copies, both were filled with terse, humorous passages and were good reading.

After spending three years making silent pictures, Will returned to Ziegfeld's Follies. In 1922 he began writing a weekly letter for the McNaught Syndicate, which soon secured a clientele of four hundred leading American newspapers for the syndicate.

As usual, he was working at several jobs at once and enjoying it. And this hard work did not blunt his humor, which was becoming keener and riper as he grew older.

POUNDING OUT HIS WEEKLY LETTER TO THE
MCNAUGHT SYNDICATE

Chapter 23
BUSY YEARS

T HE NEXT few years of Will Rogers' life were busy, crowded years. His energy seemed boundless and he was never too busy to take on new work if it interested him. In addition to writing for magazines and newspapers, as well as writing several books, he made motion pictures, talked over the radio, and was constantly being asked to speak at dinners, banquets and conventions of various kinds. He had now become a figure of national importance, and he wrote and spoke in such simple, humorous, understandable prose that people everywhere understood and loved him.

In 1923, while working near Ossining, New York, Will was a dinner guest at the home of Lewis E. Lawes, Warden of Sing Sing Prison. After dinner Will spoke to the prisoners in the chapel of the penitentiary. It was with some trepidation that he walked into the assembly room with Warden Lawes, for he was deeply sorry for the prisoners and wanted very much to make them laugh.

Another guest of the Warden that day was William J. Burns, the famous detective, and when Will Rogers got up to speak and faced the hardened, twisted countenances of the prisoners, he pointed to Burns and said:

"Don't blame me for bringin' that guy here, because I've got no more use for a cop than you have." The men laughed heartily at this.

"I hear that a lot of you are here for small stickups and robbery," he went on. "Gosh, here I've held up every theatrical producer I ever worked for and yet I'm outside! If I was in here for every dollar I've beat Ziegfeld out of, I'd be here for life." And this time the prisoners laughed even more heartily.

"He made a great hit with the men," declared Warden Lawes. "He went through the entire routine he used in the current production of the Follies."

In 1925 Will Rogers made a lecture tour under the management of Charles Wagner, and spoke to large crowds everywhere.

During this tour he was booked to make some talks in his native state, Oklahoma. He arrived at Tulsa, which had been only a wayside switch in his youth, frankly worried and apprehensive at the thought of speaking before his old friends.

"I'm scared to death," he admitted, pacing up and down his hotel room. "These old nestors will say they saw me do this same stunt on the streets at home, and now I'm holding people up for money."

Special trains ran from all over the eastern part of the state to Tulsa, and his home folks came in throngs to see him and hear him.

Will spoke before the Tulsa Shriners at noon, and as he was late in appearing, he spoke without having his lunch. "I didn't eat here," he told them with a grin, "so if I'm rotten I don't owe you anything." He also warned the Shriners to stay away from his speech that evening. "It's the strangers we want to gyp, not our friends," he declared. "I ain't after your money."

At the Convention Hall in Tulsa that night, Will worked as hard as he ever did before in his life, to please the audience. "I'll stay with you until mornin'," he promised, and gave the delighted crowd more of himself than the Follies saw in a week.

Dressed in everything from dinner jackets to cowboy hats and boots, thousands of people jammed into the hall, overflowed the stage, begging for standing room, while hundreds were turned away outside. When the audience clapped their hands, stamped and howled for more, Will told them: "That's the way with an ole' country boy . . . brag on him and he'll work himself to death. I ain't worked so hard since I stole hogs on the Verdigris."

Two hours later he paused for breath and told them this usually concluded his act. "But I want to do anything in the world you want," he said. "Perhaps if

I got my rope . . ." A roar went up at that. "I kinda feel
like I got my nerve to rope here," he went on as his
lariat sang, "If I miss, there's plenty of boys in the
audience that could come up here and show me how."

After the show Will sat on the stage and invited the
audience to come up and talk to him, and they responded
by the hundreds.

Happy with his Tulsa success, Will found the re-
mainder of the Oklahoma trip a pleasure. On reaching
Ponca City, he rushed into the "Daily News" office to
get the returns on the last baseball game of the World
Series. As he came out of the News building after the
game, a short, stubby, middle-aged Negro clapped him
on the shoulder.

"Hello, Will," he said.

"Who are you?" Will asked.

"My name's Rogahs," beamed the colored man.

"What Rogers?"

"I'm one of Rab's boys."

"Why!" exclaimed Will, a glad smile spreading over
his face, "Why, this is ole Ike! I'm shore glad to see
you." And he meant it.

"I hadn't seen him for twenty-five years," Ike Rogers
said later. "I'd heard he was comin' to town, but I didn't
know nothin' 'bout him bein' famous. I was greasy and
dirty, and scared of all them white folks, but I knowed
him the minute I seed him. I jest had to talk to him. I

couldn't help it. We visited a long time. We talked about people we knowed and the times we had as children togetheh. He gave me seventy-five dollahs, but I hadn't gone fo' money. I went because I wanted to see ole Willie."

All during the tour Will was running into old friends. At Wichita Falls he was met by Jim Minnick, his bunkmate at the old St. Louis Fair, and was whisked off for a game of polo—a game Will loved to play. Despite the fact that this day he played with borrowed equipment, and rode a strange pony, Will shot five of his team's ten goals.

When he stepped off the train at Amarillo, Texas, he looked right past the reception committee, and caught sight of Frank Ewing, friend of his old panhandle days. He made a rush for Frank and the two of them began hugging and slapping one another on the back. It was their first meeting in twenty-five years. Will had especially wanted to see Frank and had wired him: "Come to Amarillo. I made it on an old gray horse once, you ought to make it in a Ford."

Bill Johnson, of Canadian, who had sent Will from Kemper to the Ewings, was there also, and the three of them had a grand visit.

In 1926 Will went to England to appear in a motion picture—"Tiptoes"—for the British National Pictures Limited, and while there he met Lady Nancy Astor, who before her marriage was Nancy Langhorne of Virginia. Will was delighted with her and found her a busy, friendly, intelligent woman, who managed her seat in the House of Parliament with uncommon wit and pluck.

The first meeting of Lady Astor and Will Rogers occurred when Will went to the House of Commons with a letter from Charles Dana Gibson, Lady Astor's brother-in-law.

"It was during a great strike," Lady Astor relates, "and I was on my way to address a meeting of sailors and officers. I suggested that he come along with me. When I saw the size of the crowd I asked him to help me—and how he helped! He soon had that gathering rocking and roaring with laughter as he made fun of the British Navy and the American Navy, and all the things that admirals and sailors hold most dear.

"I saw at once that this man was no ordinary man. He wasn't being funny—he was funny. But under that fun there was wisdom and common sense and a love that moved mountains.

"For the next two weeks he was with us, either in our home or the House of Commons. He said he liked my coffee and he liked my husband. We treated him as a serious politician, and he met the people that we thought most worth while. His naturalness and charm fitted him for all kinds of company—and we keep all kinds of company—but I have never had better company than Will Rogers.

"I can see him now at a dinner of politicians, peers and poets, holding the table spellbound with his wit and wisdom, and occasionally looking at J. M. Barrie, the well-known English author, with an almost pitying kindness, for Barrie is a very little man and seldom laughs. But he laughed that night as I have never heard him laugh before or after. After the party was over he took Will Rogers to his flat and they talked until dawn— a thing that Barrie seldom does."

During his stay abroad in 1926, Will did a great deal of his traveling by airplane. He flew from London to Berlin and from Rome to Paris. He also made a daring dash from Berlin to Moscow in a German Fokker with a bold Russian aviator, which was probably the most exciting air ride he ever took. He described it as follows in his book "There's Not a Bathing Suit in Russia."

". . . it was piloted by the funniest old chuckle-headed, shave-haired Russian boy that didn't look like he was over twenty. But say, Bub, that clown could sure rein that thing around and make it say 'Uncle' and play dead and roll over. He was an aviator. . . . I felt her nose heading down like a bronc when he starts to swallow his head. . . .This bird could have lit on an egg and never broke it. . . . We skimmed along like a flat rock on the water, and he brought her up short and nice, like a real hand reins in a good horse."

Since his first flight in Washington, D.C., some time before, Will had become enthusiastic about airplane travel, and after that he never rode on trains or in motor cars when he could reach his destination by air. He had full confidence in foreign fliers as well as those of his own country, and demonstrated his confidence in 1926, by putting his wife and children aboard an Imperial Airways Express in Germany, for a flight to London where they were to visit friends, while he himself took a Junker plane bound for Paris.

Back in America again Will Rogers went into yet another kind of work—talking pictures. It was this medium that first carried his humor, his drawl and his unruly forelock to the nation on a wide scale. His newspaper articles were widely read, but could not record his personality. His silent pictures could not record his voice. But in talking pictures, people all over the country heard him speak and were delighted.

The Fox Company bought Homer Croy's novel, "They Had to See Paris," and realizing from the first that Will Rogers's personality was the great thing to be exploited, they wisely fitted the plot to the actor, and Will was allowed to amble along through the picture in his leisurely, homely likeable way—just being himself.

The picture was a hit, and from the start Will went

on making pictures for Fox. Soon he had the greatest earning power of any actor in talking pictures, an income that was estimated at approximately one million dollars a year. Further proof of his popularity is seen in a poll taken in 1934, among independent motion picture theater managers, which revealed that Will Rogers ranked number one, even above such stars as John Barrymore, Greta Garbo, Norma Shearer, Harold Lloyd, Dick Barthlemess and all the others, and attracted more money to the box office.

He never tried to remember his lines word for word. First, he would read the script and go over the plot with the director to get the general idea of the story. Then the cameras and sound apparatus would be started and he would handle his part in his own natural way. Frequently he would interpolate things that had never been in the script, and if they were good the director would leave them in.

If part of the action in the filming of a scene seemed unnatural to him, Will changed it. For instance, in one scene of a picture the script called for his picking up a pistol from the floor, thrusting it into his pocket and helping Dick Powell to a chair. This did not seem right to Will and he asked for a retake. Then he helped Powell to the chair before picking up the pistol, and his correction was allowed to stand.

His self-effacement in films, and his unselfishness

and willingness to surrender the spotlight to others, is recalled by Irvin S. Cobb, who appeared with Will in the film, "Steamboat 'Round the Bend." Later Mr. Cobb wrote:

"When I saw the script to the picture 'Judge Priest,' I said to myself, 'Well, Will is a great person, but after all, he's only human, and . . . he is in the acting business which is a jealous business and a tricky trade. The way this piece is written, another actor gets nearly all the final scene . . . surely Will will find a plan of shoving that other poor chap . . . into the shadows and steal the climax for himself . . .'

"What happened . . . That splendid veteran artist, Henry Walthall, carried off the last sequence, with Bill standing in the sidelines, throwing him the cues and practically effacing himself, in order to give Walthall a better opportunity to hold the center of the stage. And another result was that Walthall, who of recent years had rather faded out of prominence, was given a fat contract by somebody, on the strength of his performance in 'Judge Priest'."

Meanwhile Will's love of flying had been growing steadily. He preached aviation everywhere and always traveled by plane when he could. In the autumn of 1927, he was thrilled by a flight from Mexico City to Los Angeles with Colonel Charles Lindbergh, and a short time later he established a record by making the

"JUDGE PRIEST"—ONE OF HIS MOST SUCCESSFUL AND
APPEALING ROLES

first passenger flight from Los Angeles to New York and back to Los Angeles, in four days. He made the trip on business, and though it cost him eight hundred dollars, it saved him six full days of time.

He always championed the pilots of the planes in which he rode. Even in June, 1928, when he was flying to the Republican National Convention at Kansas City, and the right wheel of the mail plane crushed while landing at Las Vegas, New Mexico, somersaulting the machine on its back, and later that same day when the landing gear of another plane in which he was traveling, collapsed in Cherokee, Wyoming, and he was flung out, his first care was to absolve the pilots from all blame.

"Why, those fellows are the most careful flyers in the world," he pointed out. "They never purposely take a chance. I always figure their lives are worth more than mine. I've lived mine and had my fling, while I figure theirs is still ahead of them; so if they're willing to go, I am."

In 1930 and 1931, when the great drought shut down cruelly on the Southwest, Will Rogers quickly moved to help, and decided on a tour with one week spent in each of the stricken states—Texas, Oklahoma, and Arkansas.

Flying to Washington for a consultation with President Hoover and Red Cross officials, he secured the loan of a blue Curtis "Hell Diver" plane from the Naval Department, and the services of Captain Frank Hawks, as pilot. With him, as entertainers, went the Revelers' Quartette, Jimmy Rodgers, solo accordian artist, and Chester Byers, a noted roper.

The idea proved a splendid one. The opening week in Texas netted eighty-two thousand dollars, after which they moved into Oklahoma and made three appearances daily. Thanks to the speedy plane, Will and his troupe of entertainers were able to visit a number of cities in his home state, and everywhere they went the tickets were sold out and Will was warmly greeted by his audiences.

It was when he was in Stillwater, for a morning performance, that he met his old boss of the 1905 Madison Square Garden show, Colonel Zack Mulhall. The old Colonel was sick at this time and in financial difficulties, and Will previously had arranged to have him come to Stillwater for the meeting.

Walter Harrison, managing editor of the "Daily Oklahoman," told later of the meeting.

"When we arrived at the college town," he said, "the air field and the campus were jammed with people. There seemed to be no place where Will could have a minute in private. He asked me to find some place where he could talk to Colonel Zack. We cleared out a stairway, and protected the pair in it.

"Will put his arm around the old man and stuck a roll of bills the size of a baseball into the old man's pocket."

The Oklahoma tour closed at Tulsa, where Will raised twenty-nine thousand, five hundred dollars and dropped in a check of his own for five hundred dollars, to bring it up to an even thirty thousand dollars.

With one hundred and one thousand, three hundred and fifteen dollars as the week's total in Oklahoma, Will and his troupe went on into Arkansas and raised the figures for the three weeks' total to two hundred and twenty-two thousand dollars. Not only did he offer his time and services free, but he paid all expenses himself, insisting that there should be no overhead of any kind. The money all went for relief.

Chapter 24
POLO

NEXT TO roping, Will Rogers's favorite hobby was polo. He played everywhere and maintained his own stables and field on his ranch near Santa Monica, California. He was a fine shot, not a long hitter, but very accurate on either side of his horse. He was a typical cowboy rider and rode all over his horse; and how he loved to ride out an opponent!

His enthusiasm for the game drove him through chukker after chukker, at such a hot, reckless pace that once he broke a small bone in his ankle, and again a bone in his hand; and each time he played out the game.

Wearing a white uniform and with a shock of gray hair awry in the breeze, he loved nothing better than to make a long solo dash down the turf, surrounded by a gang of younger players trying to ride him off.

"Hey!" he would yell good-naturedly while riding in the heat of the game. "What's the idea of all you fellers jumpin' on me? Lay off! Lemme 'lone! What'd you wanta get on an old man for?"

Both of his boys, Will, Jr., and Jimmy, played the

C.S.WOELKER

NEXT TO ROPING, WILL ROGERS HOBBY WAS POLO

game and played it well. Will enjoyed playing with
them. And he enjoyed playing against them occasionally too. At Claremore in 1931, Will played with the
Cadets at the Oklahoma Military Academy (now Rogers State College) in an exhibition game against a
team of old-timers on whose side Will, Jr., played.

"Fine!" Will told Lieutenant Sam Houston III, the
Cadet coach, when the idea of Will and his boy playing
on opposite sides was suggested. "I been wantin' to
play against that guy for a long time."

In the contest that followed he and Will, Jr., rode
into each other like strangers, Will's team winning
nine to seven, and Will himself shooting six goals.

The polo adventure out of which Will Rogers probably got the most joy, was the time he brought the little
Oklahoma Military Academy team from his old town of
Claremore to the West Coast, to play a matched series
against the powerful Stanford team, of which Will, Jr.,
was captain.

An argument in the swanky "Uplifters Club" in
Santa Monica started it all. Cecil Smith, of Texas, had
just brought his crack polo team to the West Coast, and
had been beaten by a California team. Will contended
that Smith's team hadn't had time to become acclimated, whereupon the native sons laughed loudly.

"What do you mean, acclimated?" one of them hooted
good-naturedly. "Why California has the best polo

teams in the United States in any department. Look at our college teams—"

"College teams!" scoffed Will. "Why there's a college team back in my old home town of Claremore, that doesn't even have senior college rating, that can beat anything on the Coast!"

Naturally, the Uplifters whooped at the mention of Claremore, but soon the series was arranged. The Uplifters Club selected Stanford, champions of the Coast and the team that Will's son played on, to be matched with the team from Claremore.

Will Rogers was canny. When later he had occasion to fly through Oklahoma, he stopped off at Claremore and had a private chat with Lieutenant Houston, the Cadet coach.

"What kind of a team you got, Sam?" he asked.

"One of the best I ever had," replied the coach.

"Fine," said Will with satisfaction, "I'm liable to fix you up a little trip to the Coast."

One day he wired them to come. They secured permission from Colonel Walter E. Downs, president of the school, and hit the long trail for California. Although they were all younger boys than Stanford's, the Oklahoma Cadets were fine shots and daredevil riders who had been well coached and knew about polo tactics. Their No. 1 was Buddy Hickman, an Osage. Tommy Cross, a good interferer, played at No. 2. Tex Austin,

Jr., a tall slim boy who was a terrific hitter, lined up at No. 3, and Glen Finley, Jr., the team's captain and a great all-around player, played No. 4. Ben Saye, Powell Briscoe and Jimmy Taylor were alternates.

"Stop on the way out and play Arizona U.," Will Rogers wired them before they left. "They have an awfully good team, so use your judgment."

He was right about Arizona. They did have one of the best teams in the nation. But using the unfamiliar Arizona ponies, the Claremore team won anyhow— four to two—and Lieutenant Houston wired the result to Will Rogers.

Delighted, Will broadcast it to the world. "They're just a bunch of cowhands from Rogers County, who came out here to beat the White Britches boys," he boasted. "They ran out of gas at Tucson, Arizona, and while the tank was being filled, they went out behind the garage and beat Arizona."

All this was very amusing to the Uplifters Club members, who were backing powerful Stanford, and Will came in for more kidding. Meanwhile the Oklahoma team arrived and Will housed them in a beautiful cottage in Rustic Canyon. He gave them three days' rest, so they might get used to the horses and the climate. Quickly a string of ponies was assembled, so that both teams were evenly mounted. Will furnished the pick of his own mounts, as did Tom Guy, the manager of the club. Others were borrowed. The Claremore boys were elated with the ponies which were easily the best they ever had ridden.

The first game was played December twenty-third. Stanford's red-shirted champions went into an early lead, but riding like a band of Cheyenne raiders the young, gray-clad Oklahomans closed furiously and pulled out a ten to eight victory. Three days later the second contest come off, and although Will Rogers, Jr., hit three pretty goals and rode fiendishly, the Claremore team won again—seven to five.

Will Rogers was supremely happy. He gave the victorious squad a three-foot silver cup, and each of the seven players a fourteen-inch replica of the original. He gave the boys a one hundred dollar bill and sent them off to have a good time. Then he took Lieutenant Houston out to the Uplifters Club, and with a gleam of fun in his eyes, he paraded up and down in front of the men who, several weeks earlier, had laughed at his mention of a college team in Claremore.

"Yeah! Yeah!" he jeered, "I don't know my polo players, do I? What d'you think about that little Claremore team now?"

He poked fun at his own boy too. Cornering him, he said: "Uh huh! I told you you ought to have gone to school in Oklahoma! You might have learned how to ride and hit!"

Stanford won the third game—five to three. Will, Jr., had been moved to a scoring position and he was all over the field, making as many goals himself as the whole Cadet team.

Will Rogers did not see that game. He was making the picture, "Life Begins at Forty," but when Dr. J. C. Bushyhead of Claremore, who had accompanied the Cadets west, went to the studio and told him the result and Will, Jr.'s part in it, Will's eyes shone with pride in the achievement of his son.

Will paid all the expenses of the trip himself. It cost him twelve hundred dollars to bring the Cadets west, but he got that much fun out of it, just kidding the Uplifters. After the last game, Will brought the Oklahoma boys to his studio, let them watch him make a whole scene in the picture, took them to lunch, introduced them to everybody and, as a climax, escorted them to the Alabama-Stanford Rose Bowl football game. No wonder it was a trip the Cadets never forgot!

Although honors were thrust upon Will Rogers thick and fast, he always had the good judgment to refuse those he felt he had no business accepting. In 1928, a presidential boom for which he was in no way responsible, arose. The Rogers County Democratic convention started it and soon it had spread everywhere. But Will himself quickly blocked it.

"I certainly know that a comedian can last only till he either takes himself seriously or his audience takes him seriously," he said, "and I don't want either one of those to happen to me till I'm dead—if then. So let's stop all this foolishness right now."

Another time he was offered an honorary degree by the Oklahoma City University, but refused it. "This honorary degree thing is the hooey," he said. "I got too much respect for people who work and earn 'em to see 'em handed around to every notorious character."

His unusual stand was praised by newspapers and magazines everywhere.

As Will Rogers's popularity and earning capacity increased, his contributions to charities, both public and private, increased also. Although it is hard to obtain information on this phase of his life, because of his quietness and secrecy about it, it is known that he gave hundreds of dollars to newsboys' homes, maternity homes, hospitals for crippled children, and other institutions of like nature. During the World War he gave hundreds of dollars to the Red Cross each month, and later, in 1927, he was made a life member of this organization, a distinction of which he was very proud, for he loved the Red Cross and the work it was doing.

Eddie Cantor, the actor, once declared: "Will Rogers has Carnegie and both the Rockefellers backed off the boards in comparison. He is always giving and never telling. How much he gives away only Bill himself really can tell—and I doubt that he keeps any books on it. But I'm a poor guesser if it is less than fifty thousand dollars a year. And he'll up and deny it right, left, and center, if you accuse him of it."

It is true that Will Rogers's charities seemed endless. Through his gift of twenty-five thousand dollars to the Red Cross, which money he stipulated was to be used to support services in danger of lapsing through lack of funds, this organization was able to establish an itinerant nursing service.

Following the earthquake in southern California, Will personally contributed fifteen hundred dollars to the Red Cross relief fund. He raised more than a hundred thousand dollars for sufferers in the Mississippi flood belt and in 1929, when an appeal was made by the Red Cross for funds to help the families of sixty-one miners killed in an explosion at McAlester, Oklahoma, Will made a large personal contribution, and also aided in making a national appeal for funds.

Nor was his aid confined to his own country. In 1931, when the Nicaraguan earthquake occurred, Will flew down to Nicaragua, gave five thousand dollars, and then came back and raised another large Nicaraguan fund.

After Will Rogers's death, Admiral Cary Grayson, National Red Cross Commander, said of him:

"One is safe, in selecting the outstanding men in American life, in measuring them in terms of their attitude toward their fellow-men. By this standard, Will Rogers was truly a giant. A large percent of his personal income went for the support of charities about which the public knew little. Will Rogers loved mankind with a sincerity seldom equaled."

AT THE DEMOCRATIC CONVENTION OF 1932

Chapter 25
DEATH

LATE IN July, 1935, Will Rogers flew with his good friend, Wiley Post, to beautiful Vermejo Park in New Mexico on a vacation trip. Post, the intrepid aviator from Oklahoma, who made a record by flying around the world in a little more than seven days, was now planning to survey a possible air route between the United States and Russia, and that he was flying by way of Nome, Bering Straits and Siberia within a few days. He told Will of this plan and invited him to go along with him.

Will always had wanted to see Alaska and accepted Post's invitation enthusiastically. Back home from the fishing trip, he told his wife: "Well, Betty, I'm going to Alaska."

"Why, Will," Mrs. Rogers said, surprised, "I thought we were going east to see Mary." Mary, their only daughter, was a pretty youngster who was making good as an actress.

But Rogers, thinking of Alaska with boyish eagerness, just grinned. He could rarely be talked out of anything.

"Nope, Mother," he replied in his mild but firm way, "I've already promised Wiley."

On July 31, Post flew from Los Angeles to Seattle, where he was joined by Will. Post ordered the wheels of his plane replaced by pontoons, and when this was done the two men took off.

The plane was a Lockheed Orion-Sirius low wing that typified recent developments in aviation. It was red with silver stripes, a silvery looking three-blade propeller and pontoons, and its five hundred and fifty horsepower H-Wasp motor had a supercharger enabling the power plant to operate efficiently in high altitudes. The automatic controllable pitch propeller was designed for service at all altitudes. Upon entering thinner air, the pitch of the blades became greater, allowing even speed to be maintained. Its cruising speed was one hundred and twenty-five miles an hour, and its maximum speed, even with pontoons, was about a hundred and eighty.

They flew to Juneau in seven hours and Will got his first glimpse of Alaska. Delayed at Juneau because of bad weather, Rogers and Post finally headed for Dawson on August 9, following the Taku river and passing over Atlin and Whitehorse, and up the Yukon valley. Circling the town twice, Post brought his plane down on the swift waters of the mighty Yukon River and taxied to shore, where a large crowd of wide-eyed townspeople from Dawson were congregated to meet them.

Post stepped out first, and was quickly recognized
by the crowd because of the white patch which he
always wore over one eye. He opened the door of the

ROGERS AND WILEY POST SET OFF FOR ALASKA

plane and called, "Well, we're here," and then Will
Rogers's well-known face appeared and he stepped
down, grinning at the crowd.

"I'm just lookin' you over, boys," he called, and
everyone laughed to find him the same Will Rogers
they had so often seen in motion pictures.

The two men checked in at the Royal Alexandra
Hotel, and Will immediately hunted out every oldtimer
he could find. He had a particularly long talk with
Dawson's well-known "Apple Jimmy," who had got his
start selling apples at a dollar apiece in the old dance
hall days, and placed a generous bill in the old man's
hand when he left.

To everyone who asked Will why he was there and
where he was going, he gave the same answer: "We're
just bummin' around," he would explain. "Bummin'
here and there. We're in no hurry. Don't know where
we're goin' or how long we're stayin'—aw, ask Post. He
knows more about it than I do. I'm just thinkin' about
the good time I'm goin' to have talkin' to all these old-
timers, here in Dawson. You know—the old fellows
who came up here in '98 and know what it's really like
to get out in these hills and hunt for gold. The ones who
can tell me about the dance halls they had here, an' the
hardships they went through gettin' to this country."

When asked if Will Rogers was going to Russia with
him, Post declared: "Well, I'm going anyhow. If Will

doesn't want to go, he'll return on the boat and I'll fly to Moscow and return later. We haven't made any plans yet, but expect to spend a month and a half touring the North. It all depends on what looks interesting to us when we study the maps tonight."

Asked if he ever worried about his plane when flying over such desolate country, Post laughed. "No, I seem to have a charmed life," he said, "I'm enjoying this trip a lot, too, because I'm really seeing these towns from the ground. Other times I've just flown over them."

At Dawson, Will Rogers especially enjoyed his visit to the cabin of Robert W. Service, balladist of the North, who was then living in southern France. In the register in Service's cabin, Will wrote: "To me yours are the greatest poems ever written. Will Rogers."

He rejected an offer to take him and Post to the Matanuska valley in a "speeder car." "No," he retorted good-naturedly, "I'm not ridin' in any railroad contraption. What excuse would I have if it jumped the track and I got my neck broken? The other kinds of death are more honorable—like airplanes or falling off a horse."

From Dawson, Will and Wiley Post flew to Aklavik, on the Arctic coast of Canada, near the mouth of the MacKenzie river, and from there to Fairbanks, Alaska, by way of Herschel Island and the Porcupine River, arriving August 12.

Post made a perfect landing on the Chena River and slowly glided up-stream to the airplane float, a mile and a half from the city, where Aviator Joseph Crosson, a warm friend of both men, waited to greet them.

Will was having the time of his life, and cheerfully posed for pictures and signed autographs for all who asked him. One little girl with whom he chatted was very much of a movie fan, so when she asked Will to sign his name in her autograph book, he wrote "Clark Gable Rogers."

Getting to bed at three o'clock in the morning, Will was up again at six, strolling about the streets, with a crowd of boys and girls at his heels, and visiting informally with everyone.

"I don't want to be shown around while I'm in Fairbanks," he said, "I'll show myself around. I know pretty near everybody here, already," he added.

Will spent most of his first forenoon in Fairbanks in his hotel room, typing the daily comment and weekly letter he always did punctually for the McNaught Syndicate, and also typing answers to the telegrams he had received.

While Post's plane was being serviced by mechanics of the Pacific Alaska Airways, at Week's air field, Will and Wiley Post visited the experimental farm of the University of Alaska, where they expressed surprise at seeing the advanced growth of crops in the northern climate.

For some time Will had been looking forward to a visit to the United States Government project in the Matanuska valley, and on August 14, he, Post, Crosson and W. J. Barrows, divisional engineer, flew to this valley.

The transient workers swarmed eagerly about the plane, and Will called out to them: "Where you boys from? Anyone here from Claremore?"

They roared with laughter at that, while Will grinned. An hour and a half later, he flew away, a jest on his lips. The cook of the construction camp ran up just as the plane was ready to take off and pushed a handful of fat brown cookies into Will's hand. Will bit into one and his eyes twinkled. "They're O.K.," he shouted above the roar of the engine, "but I'll toss 'em out if we can't get off the ground!"

Back at Fairbanks, people again asked Will whether or not he was going to Russia with Post. But Will apparently had not decided. "I don't know yet," he declared. "But I do know one thing. I'm coming back to Alaska next winter. I want to get right in with the old sourdoughs, be denned up in their cabins with 'em and hear their yarns. I want to get the real low-down on 'em—be one of 'em."

Meanwhile, Post's red plane was serviced and the aviator, cautious from habit, flew to Harding Lake, fifty miles distant, where he had the fuel tanks filled to capacity. Although he thought the Chena river was large enough to take off from with a full load, Post preferred to play safe and leave from the larger surface of Harding Lake.

Their destination was Point Barrow, almost the northernmost land on the Arctic coast of Alaska. There Will wanted to meet Charles Brower, the seventy-three-year-old operator of a whaling station and trading post, who had been at Fort Barrow fifty-one years and was fancifully known in Alaska and the states as the "King of the Arctic."

But a dense fog balked them, and the careful Post postponed the departure until weather reports brought the news that conditions were better. He and Will took off from Harding Lake as soon as they received favorable reports. Despite its heavy load, the red plane lifted easily from the water and, with pontoons dripping, roared northward into the fog and clouds, its motors droning strongly.

Seven hours later, Sergeant Stanley R. Morgan, United State Signal Corps operator, stationed at Point Barrow, heard an excited babble of native voices down on the beach. Curious, he investigated and found everybody gathered around a panting Eskimo, who gasped out in broken English a strange tale of "red air plane, she blew up."

Sergeant Morgan questioned him, and as the fellow began to get his breath back, he declared he had witnessed the crash of an airplane at his sealing camp, some fifteen miles south of Point Barrow. He said the plane had come from the south, flying low, and had sighted the tents of the camp and, after circling carefully several times, had landed in a small river. There two men had climbed out, "one wearing rag on sore eye; other big man with boots, who——"

Sergeant Morgan froze with horror. The description fitted Wiley Post and Will Rogers, who everyone knew were in Alaska. Quickly he assembled a crew of fourteen Eskimos, notified a school teacher named Daugherty from the Bureau of Indian Affairs, and with the native who had run the long distance as guide, left Point Barrow in an open whaleboat powered with a small gas motor. Although the seas had opened, the boat was slowed up by ice floes and strong adverse currents. So it did not arrive at the scene of the wreck until one o'clock in the morning—more than six hours after the crash.

When the rescue party finally saw, through the fog and semi-darkness, the terribly smashed plane, their hearts chilled, for they knew what they would find. The natives had managed to cut into the cabin and extricate the body of Will Rogers, who apparently had been well back in the cabin when the plane struck, and was partially protected by the luggage. But Post's body was pinned securely by the heavy motor, which had been driven back into the cabin, and the rescuers found it much more of a task to get it out.

Carefully wrapped in eiderdown sleeping bags, found in the wreckage, the bodies were placed in a light skin boat and towed back to Point Barrow, where Dr. Henry W. Greist, Presbyterian Medical Missionary, sewed the cuts, washed the bodies and prepared them for laying out.

Meanwhile, Sergeant Morgan hurried to his radio and broadcast the tragic news that stunned the world on the morning of August 16.

The cause of the crash can never be determined, but the natives describe it as follows. Rogers and Post apparently had sighted the sailcloth tents in which the Eskimos lived in summer, and determined to ask the way to Point Barrow, although they were not far off the course. Post landed the ship, and he and Rogers got out. Will called the Eskimos to the water's edge and asked the direction. The natives pointed it out and the two men climbed back into the plane.

Then Post faced the plane about and taxied to the far side of the river for the take-off. Heading into the wind, the red ship came on, her great motors roaring evenly and powerfully. Post lifted her slowly, and when fifty feet up, banked her slightly to the right.

Suddenly there was discord in the motor's harmonious roar, then a decided break, a confused sputtering and then silence, as the crippled ship cut downward through the fog. The motor had stalled in the take-off—the thing aviators fear most, because they have no room in which to right the plane.

But Post was a fighter. As the heavily laden ship plunged toward the shallow water, the Eskimos heard a furious clicking of the controls as the aviator, keen-witted and lightning fast in the crisis, fought heroically to prevent the disaster. The plane nosed down into the water with a dull boom, smashing its right wing and turning completely over on its back.

A film of oil and gasoline floated out from the debris and slowly down the river.

Terrorized, the natives wheeled and ran, but controlling their fright they returned, and venturing timidly to the water's edge, called loudly. There was no answer, no sound at all save the slapping of the little waves against the debris of the wrecked plane.

Publisher's Note:
Many people tend to bypass an acknowledgements section, especially one as lengthy as the following, but in this case an exception should be made. This book is indeed the most definitive book ever written on Will Rogers; when you read this section, you will know why.

ACKNOWLEDGEMENTS

AS STATED in the Foreword, this book has been made possible only by the friendly aid of literally hundreds of persons. Consequently, it is an almost impossible task to give due acknowledgments. I am giving here a partial list and my grateful thanks are due not only only to these, but also to many another who helped by advice, suggestion, or stray bit of information. Thanks to them, this story of Will Rogers is a faithful picture of the boy and man, as he still lives in the minds and hearts of those who knew him best.

First I want to thank Franklin Reck, managing editor of the *American Boy,* and Joseph Brandt, director of the University of Oklahoma Press, for sound suggestions but more especially for kindling in me an enthusiasm for the project. I am indebted to Dr. M. L. Wardell, professor of history in the University of Oklahoma, for checking that portion dealing with Cherokee history. Dick Chaney, city editor of the "Vinita Daily Journal," guided me on early automobile journeys, and was so much help in other ways. To Dr. W.B. Bizzell, president of the University of Oklahoma, and to Major Lawrence "Biff" Jones, former athletic director, I am likewise indebted.

My best sources on Clem and Mary Rogers, the parents of Will, were George Mayes, John Adair, and William Gulager, all of Oklahoma. The two latter are nephews of Mary Rogers.

For information regarding a general background, I consulted Dr. J. C. Bushyhead, Gideon Morgan, Frank Goodhue Eaton, Ed Sunday, W. E. "Buck" Sunday, Susan Adair Rogers, Ed Sanders and Helen Hughes White. The most valuable sources on Will Rogers' childhood were his sister,

267

Sallie Rogers McSpadden, Gazelle Lane, Ida Mae Collins Goodale, Jeanette Billingslea and Mary Drake Strange. Much material was also gleaned from such well-informed Rogers colored folks as Agnes "Aunt Babe" Walker, Mac Walker, Anderson Rogers, and Houston, Ike, Clem, and Rose, children of Rab and Rody Rogers.

I was able to find and talk to seven people who were classmates with Will Rogers at the little Drumgoole school, Harry Jones, Bertha Glass Howard, Jenny Glass Fields, Booth McSpadden, Jack Cochran, Arch Nelms, and Bertha McSpadden Clawson; also Mrs. Martin Bell, the sister of Ida McCoy, the teacher. Four of Will Rogers' classmates at Harrell—Bluie Adair Lawrence, Dora Scott Adair Lieber, Mary McClellan Comer, and Annie Locke—told me about his life there. Information concerning the death of Mary Rogers, Will's mother, was obtained from Dr. Oliver Bagby, who attended her, and also from Gazelle and Gordon Lane, children of Dr. A. L. Lane, who also attended her.

I had difficulty establishing that Will Rogers ever attended school at Tahlequah until I met Catherine Brown Gist, at whose parents' house Will stayed while there. James Thompson and Jeter Cunningham also gave information.

Will's longest stay at any one school was at Willie Halsell College of Vinita, Okla., and I found several of his classmates in that vicinity: Marshall Stevens, Earl Walker, John McCracken, May Armstrong McCullough, Laura Stevens McClure, Oneida Cooper McCracken, Gazelle Lane, Fannie Knight Clinton, Verna Edmiston Hillin, Sam Cobb, and Browning Lewis. Also I talked to W. E. Rowsey, the superintendent at that time; Laura Cooper, the matron; and to Ellen Howard Miller, at whose home he stayed after leaving the Annex.

J. F. "Sos" McClellan and Mary McClellan Comer, the brother and sister of Charlie McClellan, gave me first-hand informa-

ACKNOWLEDGEMENTS

tion about Charlie's and Will's friendship, while information concerning his seeing the Buffalo Bill Show came from Mabel Hackney Tompkins, formerly with the show; Major Gordon W. "Pawnee Bill" Lillie, who later bought it; and several former students, at Willie Halsell College, already named, whom the boy Will Rogers told about the show.

At Neosho, Mo., home of the old Scarritt College, Leslie D. Rice helped me find many former students there with Will Rogers—Garland Price, Margaret Nay Price, Ralph Filler, Gordon Lindsey, and Harold Geyer. I also talked to Wiley Sims and Sallie Stewart and obtained other valuable material by correspondence from Wesley Knorpp, Arthur L. Perkins, Rev. Will G. Beasley, Scott Ferris, and Harry Osborne, also students at Scarritt with Mr. Rogers. Material for the Kemper chapter was gathered from John Payne, Will's roommate there, and from Ben Johnson, a fellow student. I am also indebted to Lieut. Col. A. M. Hitch for use of his excellent pamphlet, "Cadet Days of Will Rogers."

I drove to Higgins, Texas and spent several days with Frank Ewing, Will's friend there, who told me about Little Robe and the cattle drive to Kansas. I also talked to Billy Johnson's mother at Canadian, Texas. Mrs. Frank Ewing later did a lot of valuable research on this subject for which I am also grateful.

Bright Drake and A. L. "Doc" Payne, who played with Will Rogers as boys, helped with this phase of his life.

The story of Will's participation in ropings was easy to trace. I found a dozen oldtime cowboys who knew Will intimately—Jim Rider, Cullus Mayes, Joe Hogue, Heber Skinner, Jack Wright, Sam Charley, Gordon Lane, Sam Cobb, W. C. Hale, Cunnie Martin, Hick Miller, Joe Knight, and J. F. "Sos" McClellan.

Information about Will's first trip overseas came from Dick Paris, Jr., the son of Will's companion on that trip; and also from

Jim Minnick, Gordon Lane, Jim Rider, Marshall Stevens, and others with whom he later discussed it. Information concerning his early show life was obtained from Jim Minnick, who roomed with him at the St. Louis World's Fair of 1904; Charley Tompkins, his employer there; Lucille, Charley and Mildred Mulhall; Major Gordon W. "Pawnee Bill" Lillie, also an employer of Will's and Ted McSpadden, who roped with him on the stage at St. Louis. Other material was gotten by correspondence from Buck McKee, for five years Will's partner in the pony act; M. A. Shea, his first booking agent; Sam R. Leedom, of the *Sacramento Bee*; and Mary Turner.

John C. Moffitt, Noel Houston, and the Fox Film Corporation furnished information about Mr. Rogers' participation in talking pictures, while others who contributed to later chapters were Lieut. Sam Houston III, the Oklahoma Military Academy polo coach; Major Glen S. Finley, of the same school; James L. Fieser and Admiral Cary Grayson of the American Red Cross; Kermit Roosevelt, Theodore Roosevelt, Jr., Warden Lewis E. Lawes, C. B. Cochran, for whom Mr. Rogers entertained at the London Pavilion in 1926, and Lady Nancy Astor.

I am also indebted to John McCarthy, managing editor of the *Amarillo Daily News*; Mrs. Pansy Durrill; Joe Chambers, brother of Roper Blackie Chambers; Paul Muskrat; Clyde Muchmore; M. R. Cracraft; Senator Dennis Bushyhead; Charles Gilbreath for guiding me over the site of Rab Rogers' old home; Sonny Knight; Mrs. Buck McKee; Effie Powell McKee; Bruce Quisenberry, Jr.; Ben Dixon MacNeill; Jane Burnam Bolton; Mrs. Light Knight; Harold Tacker; Russell Smith, Mr. and Mrs. Ed Hicks; Eva Rider Moore, Wauhilla "Pat" Rider Fleetwood, Ruby Ann Rider Liebig, Oowala Rider Fromhals and Will Rogers Rider, Sr.

Information for the final chapter was obtained by personal correspondence with E. S. Evans, the news stories of Harriet

ACKNOWLEDGEMENTS 271

Malstrom, who interviewed Mr. Rogers and Mr. Post at Dawson, and the following Alaskan newspapers which aided generously with material and advice: *Fairbanks Daily News-Miner, Dawson Daily News, Dawson Weekly News, Alaska Daily Press;* also the Associated Press and the North American Newspaper Alliance.

I also want to thank the following for permission to paraphrase or quote material: the *Scientific American* and Carl Stearns Clancy; Harper and Brothers of New York; Albert and Charles Boni Company of New York; *Collier's Weekly* and Robert O. Scallon; the *American Magazine* and George Martin; the Bobbs-Merrill Company of Indianapolis, Ind. and Richard J. Walsh and A. B. Macdonald; the *New York Times*, Ben Dixon MacNeill; E. R. Squibb and Sons; the *Neosho Daily Democrat* and Editor Will G. Anderson, the *Springfield (Mo.) Republican, San Antonio Daily Express, Oklahoma City Times*, and *Tulsa Daily World.*

Thanks are also due James W. Moffitt and the Oklahoma Historical Society; Julia Grothaus and the San Antonio Public Library; Ruth Dolzell and the Amarillo Public Library; and Jesse Rader and the University of Oklahoma Library.

H. K.

University of Oklahoma,
July 1, 1937.
Revised Edition, October 1991